Praise for

# DECONSTRUCTING SAMMY

"Birkbeck has killer leads, gripping kickers, and sensational descriptions. This cinematic book reads more like a detective story than a traditional 'life of.'"

—*New York Times Book Review*

"Tremendous . . . Birkbeck tells the epic of Sammy Davis, Jr. . . . from his Harlem boyhood to his wrenching deathbed (he died of cancer in 1990) in his Beverly Hills mansion, where various hangers-on, seeing the circling vultures, stripped his corpse even before it was a corpse."

—*Los Angeles Times Book Review*

# A BEAUTIFUL CHILD

"Matt Birkbeck created a beautiful masterpiece."

—*True Crime Book Reviews*

# A DEADLY SECRET

"Mr. Birkbeck presents a startling inside look at the politics of police work that can place roadblocks in the place of justice."

—*Westchester County Times*

# THE QUIET DON

### The Untold Story of Mafia Kingpin Russell Bufalino

## MATT BIRKBECK

BERKLEY BOOKS, NEW YORK

THE BERKLEY PUBLISHING GROUP
Published by the Penguin Group
Penguin Group (USA)
375 Hudson Street, New York, New York 10014, USA

USA | Canada | UK | Ireland | Australia | New Zealand | India | South Africa | China

Penguin Books Ltd., Registered Offices: 80 Strand, London WC2R 0RL, England
For more information about the Penguin Group, visit penguin.com.

THE QUIET DON

A Berkley Book / published by arrangement with the author

Berkley Books are published by The Berkley Publishing Group.
BERKLEY® is a registered trademark of Penguin Group (USA).
The "B" design is a trademark of Penguin Group (USA).

For information, address: The Berkley Publishing Group,
a division of Penguin Group (USA),
375 Hudson Street, New York, New York 10014.

ISBN: 978-0-425-26685-4

PUBLISHING HISTORY
Berkley premium edition / October 2013

PRINTED IN THE UNITED STATES OF AMERICA

10  9  8  7

Cover photo by AP Photos / Bufalino.
Cover design by George Long.

*For Donna, Matthew and Christopher,*
*the loves of my life.*

# ACKNOWLEDGMENTS

A number of people helped make this book a reality, and special thanks go to my friend and former boss Peter Leffler, of the *Allentown Morning Call*, whose support and encouragement allowed me to follow this story; Nathanial Akerman, former assistant U.S. attorney in New York; Ralph "Rick" Periandi, deputy commissioner of the Pennsylvania State Police (retired); my attorney, Jay Kenoff, of Kenoff and Machtinger in Los Angeles, California, for his constructive counsel and continued support; and my editor, Natalee Rosenstein, who published my first two books and welcomed me back for a third go-round.

# PROLOGUE

———

The old man with the droopy right eye sat slumped on the witness chair pretending to be a nobody.

At five feet ten inches and nearing eighty years of age, he sure didn't look like anyone important, not with his ruffled suit and tired features. So it was hard to believe for anyone looking at him in the courtroom at the federal district courthouse in Manhattan in October 1981 that he could be a threat to anyone, much less be the man responsible for the murder of Jimmy Hoffa.

But federal prosecutors had circled around the old man following one of the most intense and thorough investigations in the history of the Federal Bureau of Investigation. More than two hundred FBI agents were assigned to the Hoffa case within hours after the former head of the Teamsters union had vanished into thin air on July 30,

1975. Over the next three years, agents conducted hundreds of interviews and reviewed countless documents, and prosecutors convened several grand juries. In addition, there were two congressional hearings and a separate Senate committee investigation. But all were frustrated and doomed to failure by the lack of evidence and the inability to get any one of the alleged conspirators to talk, chief among them the elderly man now sitting on the witness stand, who preferred to discuss the joys of dipping fresh, crisp loaves of Italian bread into a well-made tomato sauce.

So, instead, the government agents took a different tack and harassed their suspects, a small group of men long affiliated with organized crime, charging them with anything they could in the hope of pressuring them to tell the truth but otherwise feeling content that getting them off the street and inside a prison cell was an acceptable alternative.

Rosario "Russell" Bufalino was no exception.

Jack Napoli ran to the FBI seeking their protection in 1976 after Bufalino threatened to personally strangle him with his bare hands. Napoli unwisely used Bufalino's name to buy $25,000 worth of diamonds, and then bounced the check on the merchant, who subsequently sent word to Bufalino. Napoli was summoned to the Vesuvio restaurant, in midtown Manhattan, to explain himself. But it was Bufalino who did most of the talking, and everything he said, including the promise of what he would do to the six-foot-six, two-hundred-forty pound

Napoli if he didn't return the diamonds, was captured on a recording device Napoli wore, courtesy of the FBI.

"I'm going to kill you, cocksucker," Bufalino roared, "and I'm going to do it myself and I'm going to jail just for you."

Bufalino's threat was somewhat prophetic. He was indicted on federal extortion charges, found guilty and served four years in prison, where he stewed over Napoli and remained so transfixed with the informant that he enlisted a cell mate to kill him. But the FBI found out about that plan too and charged Bufalino again, this time with attempted murder as he exited the prison.

The new charges didn't bring any headlines. The media barely acknowledged Bufalino, who may have had business interests in New York, but he was, after all, from Pennsylvania of all places, which didn't warrant the often rabid media attention heaped on other organized crime figures who hailed from Manhattan, Brooklyn, Staten Island and New Jersey, such as "Crazy" Joe Gallo, Carmine Galante, Vito Genovese, Carlo Gambino and his successor, Paul Castellano.

But there were a select few who knew about the old man, and among them was Nathanial Akerman, a young assistant U.S. attorney who had been prosecuting organized crime cases for several years and had access to the sensitive files detailing Bufalino's history.

He first appeared on the FBI's radar in 1953, when his name was mentioned in a secret report filed by the Philadelphia bureau as part of the FBI's new "Top Hoodlum

Program." Over the next quarter century, Bufalino's name continually resurfaced in the FBI reports, detailing his hold over the garment industry in Pennsylvania and New York; his control over Jimmy Hoffa and the Teamsters union, especially its rich pension fund; and Bufalino's role in organizing the infamous meeting of organized crime chieftains held in Apalachin, New York, in 1957, the very meeting that finally introduced the Mafia, *La Cosa Nostra*, to America.

Akerman also had an inkling about Bufalino's connections to the plots by the Central Intelligence Agency to kill Fidel Castro.

Some twenty years earlier, in April 1961, Bufalino stood on a boat with three other men—one an agent with the CIA—that drifted in the Caribbean off the Bahamas and just ninety-miles away from where a U.S.-trained force was about to invade Cuba. Bufalino was going to follow the invaders into Havana to retrieve nearly $1 million that he had hidden just before fleeing the island more than a year earlier, after Castro consolidated his power and assumed control of the island's casinos, including two that Bufalino co-owned near Havana. Before fleeing Cuba, where he had been doing business for nearly twenty years, Bufalino had carefully wrapped the money in oilcloth and buried it. He left the island enraged, chain-smoking cigarettes as he watched the fading lights while his boat sliced through the waters of the Caribbean Sea during his hasty escape.

It was Jimmy Hoffa who had introduced Bufalino to

the CIA, in 1959, and it was Hoffa who had also been the CIA's go-between for two other gangsters, Sam Giancana and Johnny Roselli, to help in the agency's covert operation to eliminate Castro. Giancana was the powerful head of the Chicago outfit, and Roselli, from Los Angeles, began his career as a contract killer for Al Capone but left Chicago in the 1920s to oversee organized crime's control of Hollywood and later Las Vegas.

The CIA had used gangsters before, but Cuba was a natural, and tapping their anger over the loss of lucrative businesses seemed like a good idea. Cuba had long been their gold mine, gathering riches from the casinos, brothels, drugs and legitimate businesses that poured into and out of Havana. Organized crime lavished in the kind of wealth it hadn't seen since Prohibition.

Bufalino, then fifty-eight, had for years been a regular visitor to Cuba, where he had stakes in the Havana casinos, a dog track, shrimp boats and several other businesses. And he counted his success in great part to his long-standing relationship with Cuban dictator Fulgencio Batista. The two men had met in the 1940s and enjoyed a number of mutual interests, in particular a love of money.

In fact, organized crime earned more than $1 million a day from its Cuban operations. It was a joint venture with a friendly government, only now that government was gone, and in its place was an idealist and revolutionary in Castro, who initially agreed to allow the crime lords to keep their businesses but later reneged, which is why the

CIA reached out to Hoffa to enlist his organized crime partners to help eliminate the new Cuban leader.

The message was simple: President John F. Kennedy had approved air cover for a large invasion force to storm the island and ultimately overthrow Castro. But on the day of the invasion, the expected air support never materialized and the attacking force of less than two thousand CIA-trained soldiers, mostly Cuban exiles, was easily defeated. The Bay of Pigs was a military and political disaster, an embarrassment that would haunt America for decades, and Bufalino returned to the United States empty-handed.

Years had passed, and few knew the exact details of the CIA's recruitment of gangsters in its Cuban operations until 1975, when *Time* magazine reported the agency's ties to Bufalino, Giancana and Roselli. The information had spilled during a new Senate investigation led by Senator Frank Church of Idaho into the CIA's assassination efforts in Cuba and elsewhere. One *Time* story, from June 9, 1975, relayed how Bufalino and two of his associates, James Plumeri and Salvatore Granello, had left large amounts of money behind after the Communists took over.

On June 19, 1975, ten days after the *Time* story was published, Giancana was preparing a midnight snack of sausages and peppers for himself and a guest in the basement kitchen of his home in suburban Chicago. At age sixty-seven, Giancana had recently returned from a self-imposed, eight-year exile in Mexico and was far removed from the vast criminal empire he once controlled. Long replaced as the head of the Midwest mob, Giancana sought a quieter life, which included the pleasure of frying sausages in oil for a friend.

But as Giancana stood over the stove tending to his late-night meal, his visitor aimed a .22 handgun equipped with a silencer behind Giancana's head and pulled the trigger. The visitor then rolled Giancana's lifeless body over onto his back and fired six more times around Giancana's mouth.

Six weeks later, on July 30, 1975, Jimmy Hoffa sat in a suburban Detroit restaurant awaiting a visit from Tony Provenzano, a New Jersey Teamster official and highly regarded and powerful member of New York's Genovese crime family. Hoffa had been paroled by President Nixon in 1971 after serving several years in prison for conspiracy, and he was seeking to recapture the Teamsters presidency. He first needed to settle several lingering issues with Provenzano. But Provenzano never arrived, and Hoffa vanished.

A year later, on August 9, 1976, Johnny Roselli's decomposed body was found inside a fifty-five-gallon drum floating in a Florida bay. Roselli, seventy-one, had been strangled, shot and tortured. His legs had been sawed off, most likely while he was still alive.

Investigators originally believed the murders were the result of mob-related business. Organized crime figures didn't exactly welcome Giancana's return to Chicago, and Hoffa had irritated mob chieftains with his insistence in regaining the Teamsters presidency following his release from prison in 1971.

Hoffa threatened to expose their secrets at a time when organized crime's relationship with the Teamsters was never better, under the leadership of President Frank Fitzsimmons, Hoffa's handpicked successor. Tens of millions of dollars in loans from the Teamsters Central States pension fund flowed into new mob-controlled casino construction in Las Vegas and other projects, and Fitzsimmons had enjoyed a profitable relationship with President Nixon, offering his administration full Teamster support, and maintained his strong ties with the Republicans after Nixon's resignation, in 1974.

Despite warnings from high-level organized crime figures to remain in the background, the bombastic Hoffa wouldn't quit. When he disappeared, the investigators presumed he picked the wrong battle and his stubbornness led to his death.

It was the murder of Roselli that added a new, unexpected wrinkle. The Church Committee was also probing the CIA's links to the Kennedy assassination, in 1963, along with its efforts to kill foreign leaders, including Castro. During the hearings, which began in 1975, the CIA shocked the nation by surprisingly admitting to its use of gangsters to help kill Castro. The committee, seeking to learn the truth, wanted to talk to Giancana, Roselli and Hoffa.

And then came the *Time* article, which included the first-ever mention of the secretive and reclusive Bufalino.

When the committee issued its final report on the CIA's connection to organized crime, in 1976, its frustration ran deep, blaming the unsolved murders of Giancana, Hoffa and Roselli for its incomplete report and inability to discover the truth.

The CIA publicly denied any role in the murders or Hoffa's disappearance, which produced an investigation the likes of which the FBI hadn't pursued in years. Within a year, there was but a handful of chief suspects, all with affiliations either to the Teamsters or organized crime or both.

And at the top of the list was the relatively unknown figure from northeast Pennsylvania, Russell Bufalino.

So, as the old man awaited his grilling inside the federal courtroom in April 1981, Nathanial Akerman approached him wanting to talk about Hoffa and the Teamsters, about Cuba, Castro, the Kennedys and the Bay of Pigs. But the prosecutor was relegated to the case at hand, which was nothing more than Bufalino threatening to kill a nobody who used his name to steal some diamonds.

*"Now, it's true, is it not, that you are a member of* La Cosa Nostra?*"*

*"No, sir."*

*"It is true, is it not, that Carlo Gambino was a member of the* La Cosa Nostra?*"*

*"I don't know about Carlo Gambino's memberships."*

*"You knew Carlo Gambino, right?"*

*"Yes, I did."*

Akerman then showed Bufalino a photograph of Frank Sinatra standing with several men following his Septem-

ber 1976 concert at the Westchester Premier Theater, a
venue north of New York City.

"Mr. Bufalino, do you recognize anybody in this photograph?"

"I recognize Sinatra."

"Do you recognize anybody else?"

"Carlo Gambino, and this is Greg DePalma with
hair and this here is Castellano."

"That is Paul Castellano?"

"That's right."

"You also know a Mr. Angelo Bruno, do you not?"

"Yes, I do."

"Did you ever go to a meeting in Apalachin, New
York?"

"I had charge of maintenance of Canada Dry Beverage, which was owned by Mr. Joseph Barbara."

"I asked you a question. Did you ever go to a meeting
in Apalachin?"

"There was no meeting. I was called at a house there
anytime there was a breakdown or to deliver some groceries for my boss. I'd been there many times."

"Do you recall any particular date that there were a
number of people there?"

"Yes, I think sometime in November, 1959–57."

"November 14th to be exact, right?"

"I believe so."

"At that time there were a number of people that were
there, were there not?"

*"Yes, there were."*

*"And in fact Carlo Gambino was there, was he not?"*

*"I don't remember."*

*"Was Vito Genovese also there?"*

*"I don't remember."*

*"Do you know him?"*

*"Vito?"*

*"Yes."*

*"Yes, I knew Vito."*

*"Did you know him for a long time?"*

*"No, not too long."*

*"How many people were there altogether?"*

*"I don't remember. You should have the statistics."*

*"Something like fifty-eight men?"*

*"More or less."*

*"These were all people in* La Cosa Nostra?*"*

*"Not to my knowledge."*

*"You just happened to be there selling soda?" said Akerman.*

*"No," said Bufalino. "I'm a mechanic."*

Akerman smiled.

The self-described "mechanic" was a man whose unpretentious lifestyle and hidden perch in northeastern Pennsylvania served as a cover for a vast and decades-long criminal enterprise that elevated Bufalino to the top of the mob hierarchy, a figure so influential and violent, a 1964 U.S. Senate subcommittee report on "Organized Crime and Illicit Traffic in Narcotics" described Bufalino as "one of the most ruthless and powerful leaders of the Mafia in the United States."

To those who knew him very well, including Akerman, Russell Bufalino was arguably the most powerful organized crime figure in the nation.

"So," said Akerman. "You're a mechanic?"

"That's right," said Bufalino.

# ONE

Two Pennsylvania State Police troopers sat inside an unmarked car waiting for the go-ahead to do something they had never done before, arrest a Catholic priest for lying to a grand jury.

It was early January 2008, and the troopers, Rich Weinstock and Dave Swartz, had been waiting for nearly an hour with the engine off, the cold morning air laying a thin frost on the windows.

The Rev. Joseph Sica was inside the St. Mary of the Assumption Church monastery, likely having breakfast. He usually left just before 9 A.M. for Mercy Hospital, where he was the resident chaplain, and the troopers had planned to arrest him before he left for work. When the call finally came, just after 8:30 A.M., the troopers exited the car and walked briskly to Sica's front door. He lived in an apartment at the monastery, which was in Scranton, and after several knocks, the door opened and there stood the burly priest, somewhat surprised that he had two guests so early in the morning.

"Father Joseph Sica, I'm Trooper Weinstock, this is Detective Swartz. We are with the Pennsylvania State Police and we have a warrant for your arrest."

Sica was stunned. He had seen the troopers before, during the grand jury hearings in Harrisburg the previous summer. But he was just a witness and not the target of the investigation. When Sica asked why he was being arrested, he was told he was being charged with perjury.

Weinstock handcuffed Sica and sat him on a chair and informed him he had a search warrant. Within minutes, the troopers found a handgun and $1,000 in cash.

"I have a permit for that," said Sica of the gun. Irate, the priest threatened Weinstock, telling him that he was opening himself to exposure of a sexual harassment lawsuit filed by a female trooper. The complaint had been dismissed, so the priest's threat meant nothing.

The troopers put a coat over Sica's shoulders and led him to the police cruiser. Several other troopers had arrived to mop up as Sica was put in the backseat for the two-hour drive to Harrisburg.

Within minutes, a fidgety Sica said he had to make a call, and he asked Weinstock if he could use his cell phone.

"Who you calling?"

"A friend. I have to notify my attorney."

Intrigued, Weinstock pulled out his phone, and Sica rattled off a phone number, after which Weinstock reached back and put the phone to Sica's ear and mouth. The volume was on high, so the troopers could hear the phone ring and the gruff voice that answered.

"Lou, it's me. Listen, I've been arrested."

"You what?"

"I've been arrested. They're taking me now to Harrisburg."

"Don't say anything. We'll take care of it, you hear me?"

"Yes."

"Where are you now?"

"I'm in the police car. I'm with the troopers. They're taking me to jail in Harrisburg."

"You're what, inside the car now talking to me? Get off! Get off the phone!"

Weinstock and Swartz heard everything, including the abrupt hang up, and they recognized the voice on the other end of the line.

"You called DeNaples?" said Weinstock.

IT WAS ALMOST three years earlier, in April 2005, when Ralph Periandi was thumbing through more than a dozen files sitting on his lap on the drive back to the Pennsylvania State Police headquarters, in Harrisburg, from Philadelphia, reviewing his notes from his meeting with the FBI.

Periandi was a lieutenant colonel and a deputy commissioner, which was the second-highest rank within the state police and just one step below the commissioner. Of medium height, clean-cut, his gray uniform pressed to perfection and hair buzz-cut short over a trim and fit figure, Periandi looked the part of a police commander, and he had dressed to make an impression.

For nearly thirty years, he enjoyed a career that took him to different posts throughout the state, from a fresh-faced trooper writing speeding tickets outside Philadelphia in 1975 to running the Bureau of Criminal Investigations (BCI), a prestigious post where he commanded the nerve center for all state police investigations. As a major in charge of BCI, Periandi had his finger on the pulse of crime in the state, and it was from that platform that now, as deputy commissioner, he decided he could commence a probe of Pennsylvania's popular governor, Ed Rendell and his administration, which was the primary reason for the meeting with the FBI.

Rendell had been elected governor in November 2002. He was a rare force of will and personality who, as Philadelphia's mayor in the 1990s, had gained national acclaim for leading that city's remarkable transformation. Originally from New York, Rendell attended college in Philadelphia, first at the University of Pennsylvania, and then law school at Villanova. Following graduation, he remained in Philadelphia and served as an assistant district attorney before diving into politics and winning. He won his first political race in 1977 using an anticorruption platform to defeat the incumbent district attorney.

Rendell served two terms as district attorney before making an ill-fated run for governor in 1986. He lost his first bid for mayor of Philadelphia but won on his second try, in 1991, and took over the administration of a crime-ridden, nearly bankrupt city with deep divisions within its multiethnic constituency. But by the time he left office, in 1999, he had led a stunning turnaround, turning a budget deficit into a surplus and, through sheer will and political cunning, erased Philadelphia's negative national perception and replaced it with a burgeoning pride.

Despite his success, Rendell never took his eyes off his main prize, the governorship, and he resigned as mayor in late 1999 to take up the chairmanship of the Democratic National Committee (DNC), a post he held during the 2000 presidential election and the chaotic weeks that followed as the courts decided the historic outcome between Republican George W. Bush and Democrat Al Gore.

But Rendell's tenure in Washington, D.C., was a temporary diversion as he plotted his next major political conquest, which became apparent to all after he resigned as DNC chairman in 2001 to focus on the 2002 Pennsylvania gubernatorial election.

The post had been held by two-term Republican governor Tom Ridge, but he resigned following the September 11, 2001, terrorist attacks on New York, Washington, D.C., and Pennsylvania to accept the appointment as head of a brand-new federal agency, the Department of Homeland Security.

After announcing his candidacy, Rendell created a campaign strategy that used as its centerpiece the successful legalization of casino gambling. For years, Pennsylvania property owners fell victim to spiraling school property taxes, which crippled many of state's cities and municipalities. Feeding off voter anger, Rendell devised his *Plan for a New Pennsylvania*, which would seek legislative approval of slots machines by arguing that the $1.5 billion in expected proceeds would be distributed to school districts to lower property taxes. The initial idea was to allow gambling at horse tracks, but to reach the $1 billion mark and above, the state had to license several stand-alone casinos. The idea was universally rejected.

Gaming had for decades been seen as a panacea for curing many of Pennsylvania's ills, but it never garnered much support from voters or the legislature. For his part, Rendell pointed to table games in Atlantic City, slots in West Virginia as well as gambling initiatives in other nearby states, such as Maryland, Delaware and New York, and argued that if Pennsylvania didn't get in the mix now, it would be shut out and forever lose billions in potential tax revenues.

Despite Rendell's pleas, the public remained decidedly against the initiative, as did a majority of elected officials, including the Republicans and most Democrats in the state legislature in Harrisburg. But that didn't stop Rendell from working behind the scenes with two of the state's most powerful lawmakers, Democratic senators Vincent Fumo, of Philadelphia, and Robert Mellow, who represented a large portion of northeast Pennsylvania, including Scranton.

The two lawmakers had for years served as the major power brokers within Pennsylvania state politics but were forced to take backseats during the seven years of Republican leadership under Ridge, who did his best to eliminate many of the "perks" within Harrisburg politics. In one instance, Ridge put the kibosh on a long-standing secretive agreement that traditionally offered control of the Pennsylvania Turnpike Commission (PTC) to the party in power. The PTC oversaw and administered the hundreds of miles of Pennsylvania highway, from east to west and north to south, with the toll road serving as a feeding ground for greedy politicos who received large contributions and even side cash from a deep well of individuals and businesses eager to gain a share of the billions in state contracts. Those favored somehow got the choice assignments, including the handful of major law firms in Philadelphia, Harrisburg and Pittsburgh that won lucrative contracts as counsel to PTC bond issues.

Unbeknownst to Pennsylvania's populace, and to most legislators, there had been for years a gentlemen's agreement within the legislative leadership that stipulated the party in power controlled 50 percent of all Turnpike contracts, while the other 50 percent was split between the minority party and the governor.

The exception to the agreement was Tom Ridge, a conservative Republican from Erie with designs on the U.S. presidency who tried to limit the patronage that long overwhelmed the state capital. Ridge's efforts muted the deal making, especially at the PTC.

Rendell won the 2002 election comfortably, and the subsequent Democratic takeover of the House and Senate opened the doors wide to resume the previous practices. Especially for Fumo, who had been the autocratic ruler of the state capital and the most influential legislator in Harrisburg. Fumo's network reached far beyond government to the most powerful law firms and corporations doing business in Pennsylvania, and his reach also infiltrated the state Supreme Court, which had at times been criticized for putting politics before the law.

Following his election win, Rendell immediately tasked Fumo and Mellow with initiating a report on the potential for gaming legislation. When it was submitted to the Senate Democratic Appropriations Committee, in mid-2003, the "Pennsylvania Slot Machine Facilities: State-wide Revenue Projections" report suggested six so-called racinos and six stand-alone casinos for Pennsylvania, with two in Philadelphia, one in Pittsburgh, one near Pocono International Raceway in Long Pond and two undetermined locations, most likely Allentown and Shrewsbury. The report suggested a one-time $50 million licensing fee for successful applicants, with the state taking 34 percent of all gross daily receipts. The market potential, according to the report, was nearly $3 billion, with more than $1 billion going to state coffers to help weary taxpayers.

Although the plan failed to capture the support of the public, by early 2004, the gaming initiative was moving full speed ahead behind the scenes within legislative circles. For deputy state police commissioner Ralph Periandi's purposes, early meetings with the Rendell administration had produced a blueprint that would include the state police in the vital role of casino security and the ultra-important role of conducting background investigations of potential casino owners, along with other key personnel and employees. Neither Periandi nor his boss, commissioner Jeffrey Miller, were in favor of the measure, with both men sharing the belief that gaming would attract a bad element. Many legislators, mostly Republicans, shared their negative opinions, and their opposition to the legislation delayed a vote, while Democrats horse-traded with their own leadership. The Philadelphia black caucus, for instance, refused to support the legislation unless one of the casino licenses was awarded to an African-American. The caucus also insisted that an African-American was appointed to what would be the seven-member Pennsylvania Gaming Control Board responsible to oversee the new initiative.

Despite the overwhelming public opposition, the arm-twisting and negotiating continued until legislators were called to a bizarre midnight vote on July 4, 2004. When it was originally introduced, the legislation was a thirty-three-line document about background checks at state horse tracks. Fumo's staff spent weeks rewriting the bill, and when it emerged from the Senate on July 1, 2004, it was now one hundred and forty-five pages long.

Known as the Pennsylvania Race Horse Development and Gaming Act, and commonly known as Act 71, the bill authorized slots gambling throughout the state and paved the way for 61,000 slot machines at fourteen casinos at yet-to-be determined sites. Table games, such as blackjack and poker, weren't included in the bill, though there was an understanding those games would eventually be part of the mix. Debate on the bill began on Saturday, July 3, and the voting went down party lines, with

Rendell, Fumo and Mellow pressing hard on the Republican majority in the House and Senate, which followed its leadership and approved the legislation.

Pennsylvania had casino gambling, and Periandi had his antenna up.

Miller had been on vacation that holiday weekend in Ocean City, Maryland, but at the behest of Rendell spent most of his time on the phone assuring fence-sitting legislators that the police supported the initiative. Both Miller and Periandi were Rendell appointees, and the reality of the situation called for Miller, as commissioner, to follow the administration's lead. But privately, both Miller and Periandi had grave doubts about the legislation, and it took just a few weeks for those doubts to be confirmed, but in a way Periandi never imagined.

Just a week after the vote, the police were summoned to a closed-door meeting with John Estey, Rendell's chief of staff, and Greg Fajt, the secretary of the Department of Revenue, which was the agency charged with overseeing the early creation of the new gaming initiative. Estey and Fajt said that Rendell expected quick clearances on background checks of favored Rendell appointments to the newly created Gaming Control Board. Included among them was Frank Friel, a former Philadelphia police officer whom Rendell appointed as the gaming board's first chairman. In addition, there would be several favored candidates applying for slots licenses. Among the names mentioned was Louis DeNaples, an immensely powerful businessman from the Scranton area with deep political ties and long-rumored associations with organized crime who had coincidently just announced his intention to buy the shuttered Mount Airy Lodge Resort in the Poconos and apply for a slots license.

"We're not going to have any problems with this," said Estey, directing his command to the state police liaison, Captain Ron Petyak.

After receiving the edict from Estey, Petyak went back to Periandi with the disturbing news.

"This is not what you think this is. It's a setup," said Petyak. "I think this is a scam and we're being used."

Periandi and Petyak immediately went to Miller, and his response was measured, acknowledging Petyak's concerns but telling him and Periandi to stay the course and follow the administration's lead.

"You should also know the governor is going to appoint Frank Friel as the gaming board chairman. He has a problem," said Periandi.

"You're kidding," said a surprised Miller.

"No, I'm not. I already know some of the issues and you may want to let the governor's office know it may not be smooth sailing," said Periandi.

Friel once headed Philadelphia's Organized Crime Task Force and had claimed that during his tenure, he played a key role in prosecuting members of that city's Mafia in the 1970s. But Periandi knew from his days heading BCI that Friel had been closely watched by internal affairs after police learned of his friendship with a boxing promoter with alleged mob ties. Friel had also allegedly misrepresented his academic credentials and had been named in a 1974 Pennsylvania Crime Commission report as being one of a group of police officers who allegedly took bribes from a Philadelphia club owner.

Miller again told his subordinates to stay the course, and Friel was appointed gaming board chairman on August 11, after which he submitted a background questionnaire that was short on his personal details. So Periandi ordered his detectives to reinterview Friel and dig into his past. The detectives ran down leads but always seemed to be half-a-step behind the press, which had also taken an interest in Friel, particularly the Philadelphia media.

To keep their information secure and help the administration avoid a potentially embarrassing controversy, Periandi suggested that the state police simply make a recommendation as to Friel's fitness to hold the position. The administration nixed that idea, and Friel remained the chairman. But when the background investigation was completed, just after Labor Day 2004, Periandi went to Miller with the grim news.

"The administration will be concerned if this Friel report gets out," said Periandi. "I think the way to get around this is for the administration to tell Friel to step back from the appointment."

Miller brought the suggestion to Rendell, and the reply was swift: Friel would not step aside. In addition, Rendell wanted to see the full state police report. But the allegations, which were supposed to be confidential, surfaced in the *Philadelphia Daily News*, and Friel, who vehemently denied any wrongdoing, was forced to step down as chairman less than a month after he was appointed.

Friel's resignation infuriated Rendell, who during an emotional press conference publicly lashed out at the media for publicizing the allegations.

"You've unfairly tarnished the reputation of a good and decent man," said Rendell, with tears in his eyes. "I hope you understand what you did."

But it wasn't the media that drew Rendell's wrath. Privately, he seethed at the state police and blamed the police for leaking their report. It was a fiasco that not only embarrassed the administration, but created much larger problems for future Rendell appointments. If Rendell's first gaming appointment could easily get blown out of the water, how would other favorite candidates and appointees with checkered histories pass police muster, especially those seeking gaming licenses, such as Louis DeNaples? The solution came in a report that Greg Fajt and the Department of Revenue had commissioned from a consultant six months earlier.

Spectrum Gaming was a New Jersey firm headed by Fred Gushin, a respected gaming authority and a former New Jersey assistant attorney general. Tasked by Fajt and the Rendell administration with creating the foundation of the new gaming industry, Gushin produced a "Blueprint for Gaming." The one-hundred-plus-page report was submitted in October 2004, and among Gushin's many recommendations was tasking the state police with overseeing the all-important background checks. But just days after submitting his report, Gushin was told to immediately stop work and turn over all documents relating to its assignment. No one knew what was going on until

December, when Gushin learned that Fajt had changed his report. Among Fajt's recommendations was the creation of a new agency—the Bureau of Investigations and Enforcement (BIE)—that would be under the control of the gaming board, and would supplant the state police and conduct all background checks. The police role was reduced to performing low-level background checks and overseeing casino security.

Gushin was furious that the administration would pass off the new recommendation as his work product, and he fired off a letter on December 9, 2004, to the new gaming board chairman-designate Thomas "Tad" Decker, a well-connected attorney and partner with the powerful Philadelphia law firm Cozen O'Connor.

"This report does not reflect our work product and we do not concur in its recommendations and conclusions," wrote Gushin.

The decision to replace the state police with BIE also stunned Periandi and Miller. Their relationship with Fajt had grown cold, but they had no idea just how frosty it had become. In retrospect, although they thought they were doing their jobs in ferreting out Friel, they derailed Rendell's first nomination, which was a mistake the governor wouldn't make twice. By giving background investigations to BIE, the gaming board would effectively control the investigative process, especially for favored casino applicants. But BIE was a civilian agency, and even though it would be stocked with former law enforcement personnel, they would not be privy to the kind of deep, classified criminal information available only to law enforcement agencies, such as the state police or FBI.

That meant anyone applying for a gaming license in Pennsylvania would not be fully vetted.

It was a disaster in the making, and none of this made any sense to Periandi. And as he pondered the administration's actions, another unsettling issue was developing, and this one had to do with Louis DeNaples.

# Two

Once a jewel that for decades drew vacationers from the New York metropolitan area eager to lap up the country air, good food and celebrity entertainment, Mount Airy Lodge had, by the 1990s, lost its luster. Plagued by financial difficulties, the resort closed in 2001 after its owner committed suicide, and it was taken over by a private-equity firm, Cerberus Capital Management, which later sold it to Louis DeNaples, in 2004.

Periandi first heard about DeNaples in the early 1980s, when his name surfaced in several Pennsylvania Crime Commission reports. DeNaples, according to the reports, had close associations with the Bufalino crime family, which in its heyday was only fifty members strong yet controlled all organized crime activity in northeast Pennsylvania and parts of southern New York State. Among its favored businesses were loan sharking, extortion, money laundering, labor racketeering and prostitution.

According to the crime commission reports, DeNaples' relationship with the Bufalinos was publicly unveiled after he pleaded no contest in 1978 for defrauding the U.S. government for taking part in a scheme that fraudulently billed more than $500,000 for supposed cleanup work from Hurricane Agnes, which devastated the region in 1972. DeNaples was charged with several other men, including Scranton city officials, but the trial ended in a hung jury, with one lone holdout forcing an acquittal. Prior to a second trial, DeNaples pleaded no contest to a single fraud charge. He paid a $10,000 fine and was placed on probation but escaped a prison sentence.

But in 1980, the FBI was tipped off that the first De-Naples' trial had been fixed by several members of the Bufalino family, among them James Osticco, the underboss and a hard-core gangster whose relationship with the family namesake, Russell Bufalino, went back to the 1950s. Both men had been arrested at the famed mob gathering in Apalachin, New York, in November 1957, which for the first time brought organized crime out into the national public eye.

In 1983, Osticco and several others were tried and convicted for bribing the juror and her husband. The price was cheap: $1,000, a set of car tires and a pocket watch.

The DeNaples case was subsequently referenced in several Pennsylvania Crime Commission reports, as were his alleged ties to Osticco and several other organized crime figures, among them William D'Elia, who had taken over leadership of the Bufalino family in the mid-1990s.

The DeNaples story was the legendary rags to riches. His father, Patrick, was a railroad worker, and DeNaples grew up piss poor, sharing shoes and other clothing with his siblings. As a young man, he sold Christmas trees on a corner lot, using his profits to buy a single junked auto. Some forty years later, DeNaples led a billion-dollar legacy that included ownership of two of the largest garbage landfills in Pennsylvania and several auto junkyards and appointments to some of the region's most prestigious boards, including the University of Scranton and Blue Cross Blue Shield, where he rubbed elbows with some of the most-respected and well-known names in the region. He also had his own bank, First National Community Bank, where he served as chairman and was the largest stockholder.

By the 1990s, everyone in the region and in the wide halls of the capital in Harrisburg knew about DeNaples, who aside from being a shrewd businessman attended mass daily and was a major benefactor who gave away millions to local charities and the Catholic Church. DeNaples' donations were legendary, including a $35 million gift to the University of Scranton for a gleaming marble building named after DeNaples' parents. His philanthropy helped him gain wide support among not just the local populace, but the entire political infrastructure. DeNaples also cultivated deep ties within state and federal government and counted figures such as Pennsylvania senator Arlen Specter as friends. He also had well-entrenched associations with law enforcement, so few people dared oppose him.

As Periandi ascended through the police ranks, he would often hear about DeNaples, but not for his charitable pursuits. Aside from the Pennsylvania Crime Commission reports, DeNaples' name had surfaced on occasion. In 2001, a federal affidavit directly connected him to William D'Elia. Known as "Big Billy" for his hulking six-feet-four-inch frame, D'Elia was once Russell Bufalino's driver and bodyguard whose notoriety earned him a lifetime ban in 2003 from the New Jersey Division of Gaming Enforcement from entering any Atlantic City casinos.

Following Bufalino's death, in 1994, it was D'Elia who eventually gained control of the family, and according to the 2001 affidavit, several confidential informants alleged that DeNaples had made payments to D'Elia for undisclosed work and protection. No charges were filed against D'Elia or DeNaples in connection with this investigation.

Periandi had enough of a working understanding of DeNaples to know of his wide influence within the state, particularly its political circles, and he was disturbed that DeNaples was seeking a gaming license. Even more disconcerting was the language in the new gaming legislation, which barred convicted felons from owning casinos unless the conviction was older than fifteen years. DeNaples' 1978 conviction, ironically, was more than twenty-five years old, which qualified him for a license in Pennsylvania but not in other gaming states, such as Nevada or New Jersey. In addition, Periandi couldn't help but notice that DeNaples' purchased the Mount Airy property *before* he was even approved for a slots license.

Something was clearly amiss, and no doubt, Periandi believed, the DeNaples entrée into gaming was one of the primary reasons why the state police were cast aside: DeNaples was certain to get a slots license. Given DeNaples' history, Periandi believed that a routine state police investigation should have blocked any chance of him owning a casino. But with the police now out of the picture, there was nothing to stop the gaming board from eventually granting DeNaples a casino license.

But to make that happen and gain final approval for DeNaples and any other potential licensee with a questionable history supported by the Rendell administration, Periandi theorized that it required the participation from not only the gaming board, but possibly the leaders of the state legislature and the Rendell administration.

By 2005, as the state was moving ahead with its gaming initiative, Periandi felt more uncomfortable with the entire effort and decided it was time to take a closer look. But he needed a partner. The dichotomy of Pennsylvania state politics afforded few secrets, even within law enforcement. Periandi didn't have any faith in the state attorney general's office, which no doubt would have quickly signaled to Rendell that something was afoot. At best, the understaffed attorney general's office would simply have meddled in the probe and produced a half-assed investigation that may have resulted in a few allegations but end with no charges.

Periandi also had issues with the U.S. attorney's office

in Harrisburg, which was part of the Middle District, which included Scranton and Wilkes-Barre, DeNaples' home turf. So Periandi made a single phone call, and on April 28, 2005, he left his office in Harrisburg and headed to FBI headquarters in Philadelphia.

When he arrived, waiting for him inside a large conference room were Jack Eckenrode, the senior special agent in the Philadelphia office, and John Terry, the special agent in charge of public corruption. Joining them were half a dozen other special agents from Philadelphia, Pittsburgh, Harrisburg, Erie and Scranton. Eckenrode quickly gave the floor to Periandi, who opened the meeting by explaining how he suspected that Rendell, members of his administration and others in state government might be trying to control the new gaming industry in Pennsylvania.

Periandi recapped the previous twelve months, including the Friel investigation, and to further make his point, he said that just two days earlier he and Petyak had met with members of the Gaming Control Board, including its chairman, Tad Decker, to again discuss the future state police role. But Decker and the board had little use for the police and made it clear, again, that the gaming board would rely on its own BIE for critical background investigations of all casino applicants. Of particular interest to Periandi was the sudden addition of attorney William Conaboy to the gaming board. Conaboy was one of De-Naples' attorneys in Scranton and had served on several boards with him.

Periandi said he had also become aware of another potential issue. The Rendell administration had hired a

Rhode Island firm, G-Tech, to oversee the implementation of the central computer system that would eventually have primary control over each of the sixty thousand slot machines in the state. The contract to create and oversee the computer system ran into the tens of millions of dollars, and Periandi was floored when he learned that G-Tech was populated with executives who previously served in high positions under Rendell when he chaired the Democratic National Committee (DNC). Among them was Donald Sweitzer, a G-Tech vice president who was a twenty-year member of the DNC and its former political director and a fund-raiser. And Kenneth Jarin, a fund-raising chairman for the DNC, was hired by G-Tech as a consultant. Jarin was one of Rendell's partners at his old Philadelphia law firm Ballard Spahr and a close aide who was Rendell's biggest fund-raiser for his 2002 gubernatorial run.

Given the numerous players involved, Periandi said he couldn't conduct a public corruption probe of this magnitude on his own. He just didn't know how deep into the rabbit hole he'd have to dig to potentially flush it out, and he needed the FBI to be a partner. The state police would do the heavy lifting, Periandi said, and he even surprised those in the room with the disclosure that he had his own "Black Ops" team of covert investigators that reported directly to him. No one outside of Periandi's small group would know about the investigation, he said, not even the commissioner, whom Periandi said required "plausible deniability."

"If we establish a lead but can't pursue it, then I want to know I can turn to you to run with it," Periandi said.

To Periandi's surprise, Eckenrode agreed. The FBI, said Eckenrode, had already initiated its own public corruption probe of Pennsylvania politicians. Eckenrode wouldn't disclose who was under investigation, but he shared Periandi's opinion there were major concerns with the gaming initiative and a joint effort would be beneficial to both the state police and FBI. Periandi did not know if the FBI was looking at Rendell, but the most likely candidates were members of the state legislature, perhaps Vince Fumo. Periandi knew, for instance, that the long-time Senate leader had several prior unpublicized brushes with the law, including a state police investigation into falsified applications to the state Liquor Control Board from several nonprofits with ties to Fumo. The FBI had also been looking into the matter, which prompted Periandi and the state police to move aside.

There was also Robert Mellow, who had been a member of the Senate since the 1980s and, like Fumo, had integrity issues. Periandi became familiar with Mellow from his days serving as commander of Troop N, a busy hub in Hazleton that oversaw much of northeastern Pennsylvania, from the Poconos up through Scranton and Wilkes-Barre, which was part of Mellow's district.

Mellow had once been under federal investigation for allegedly taking kickbacks from Mount Airy Lodge during the 1980s, though no charges were ever filed. He was also a very close confidant of Louis DeNaples. They were so close that the two men would meet regularly, often going for private walks to discuss business and other matters of interest.

With the FBI on board, the task force was formed, and Periandi would quietly begin his investigation, with Governor Ed Rendell and his administration as the chief targets. Upon returning to Harrisburg, Periandi immediately shared the news with his small "Black Ops" team, which included one of his most-trusted members, trooper Richie Weinstock.

Weinstock was a former narcotics detective who was handpicked by Ron Petyak as an original member of the state police gaming intelligence unit that was formed after the legislation was passed, in July 2004. Weinstock had grown up in the Scranton area, and he knew the history of the region, including the wide influence of the Bufalino family. Lackawanna and Luzerne Counties, home to Scranton and Wilkes-Barre, respectively, were by even the lowest of standards places where corruption was endemic and an accepted part of everyday life. From the old Kefauver Committee of the 1950s, one of the early federal investigations into organized crime that determined law enforcement in the region to be utterly "blind" when it came to prosecuting gambling, to the later convictions of major political figures such as the popular congressman Daniel Flood, of Wilkes-Barre, in the 1970s for taking payoffs, and the state attorney general Ernie Preate, of Lackawanna County, in 1995 for mail fraud.

The entire region, from Scranton to Wilkes-Barre, had

long been thought to have operated in its own vacuum, where the crooks were the good guys and everyone else looked the other way.

Weinstock was a charmer, with a loud, outgoing personality and intensity and talent for detective work. It was Weinstock whom Periandi first tasked with quietly conducting secret background checks on members of the Rendell administration, including John Estey and Greg Fajt, after the gaming legislation was approved. Apprised of the new probe, Weinstock was given strict orders that the gaming investigation would be "off the line," meaning there was no direct chain of command other than he reported to Petyak, who reported to Periandi.

Nearly three years later, the fruits of that investigation began to bear out with the stunning indictment of the Rev. Joseph Sica, who was charged with lying to a grand jury impaneled the previous summer in Harrisburg to investigate DeNaples and determine if he had lied to the gaming board about his mob ties.

As expected, DeNaples had been awarded a slots license in December 2006, despite warnings from Periandi to Tad Decker and the gaming board that there were issues. Periandi couldn't say why, so the board ignored him and went ahead and approved DeNaples anyway. Two months later, the state police took their case to Ed Marsico, the district attorney for Dauphin County in Harrisburg, who impaneled the grand jury in April 2007 to investigate whether DeNaples lied to the gaming board about his alleged mob ties.

Marsico's first assistant, Fran Chardo, headed the prosecution, but the first charges would be filed against Sica, a tangential figure at best but someone who could claim close associations to both DeNaples and to Russell Bufalino. During and after his bid for a casino license, the gruff DeNaples would appear at public hearings with Sica at his side, a strange sight, given that the burly Sica acted more like a bodyguard than a spiritual advisor, clearing the way through masses of people, particularly a hungry press eager to hear from the secretive DeNaples. Despite Sica's denials, the grand jury also learned that the priest and the old don had been very close, so close that Bufalino attended Sica's ordination party some twenty-five years earlier.

Less than a month after Sica was indicted, DeNaples was charged with lying to the gaming board about his relationship with Billy D'Elia and about his past ties to Bufalino.

The grand jury had heard testimony from D'Elia, who was imprisoned awaiting trial on charges of money laundering and conspiracy to kill a witness when he testified about his "friend Lou" in July 2007. He and DeNaples were so close, said D'Elia, that DeNaples attended his daughter's wedding in 1999, along with several gangsters from Philadelphia, including "Skinny" Joe Merlino.

D'Elia also testified before the grand jury about De-Naples' close friendship with Bufalino, and how they were together at dinners and boxing matches, and how Bufalino underlings often visited with DeNaples at his office at his auto parts store.

DeNaples' indictment on January 30, 2008, was announced inside the capital by Marsico and state police commissioner Miller. Marsico quickly impaneled another grand jury, with this one set to probe the gaming board, particularly its former chairman Tad Decker, with the expectation that it would lead to the investigation's original targets, Governor Ed Rendell and his administration.

But less than a week after DeNaples was charged, the state Supreme Court interceded in the case and stopped the prosecution, enlisting its rarely used "Kings Bench" powers to stay the case. Prosecutors vehemently protested, arguing that the court's use of Kings Bench was highly inappropriate and had never been used before in a criminal case. But the decision stuck, and the investigations against DeNaples and the gaming board would remain in limbo for the foreseeable future.

The Supreme Court had interfered in the case before, and its continual interference raised a number of red flags, and the police and prosecutors were more than puzzled over why the justices would step in on behalf of a man with alleged long-standing ties to organized crime. A year earlier, the same court upheld the state gaming board's decision to award DeNaples a casino license after one of his competitors filed suit claiming DeNaples received preferential treatment from the board and the governor.

Greg Matzel, a New Jersey home builder, had partnered with Morris Bailey, a billionaire New York developer, to buy Pocono Manor, an old Pennsylvania resort situated just a few miles from DeNaples' Mount Airy Casino Resort. With access to two highways, Matzel and

Bailey presented a plan for a new "destination resort" complete with a casino, eighteen-story hotel, golf courses, shopping center, sports arena and convention center. The plan was far more ambitious than the one DeNaples presented and promised more revenue, yet the gaming board chose DeNaples, and the decision was later upheld by the Supreme Court.

Now, the widening investigation into DeNaples and the gaming board was unexpectedly stopped by the state's highest authority, and after several weeks of discussion among the police and prosecutors, all wondered if the highest court in the state was part of a conspiracy. And, if so, did DeNaples truly wield the kind of power that would influence an entire state government and its courts?

The men asking the questions believed they knew the answers. What they didn't know was why and how. Why would the Rendell administration take part in such an elaborate subterfuge, and had someone like Louis De-Naples become such a titular figure that even the courts would bend to him?

To help find the answers, the troopers were dispatched to reinterview the many witnesses who testified before the grand jury, and first on their list was Billy D'Elia. When they arrived at the prison, Weinstock said they needed to talk.

"What about?" said D'Elia

The police explained their frustrations, and the discussion quickly turned to Russell Bufalino. The police and the mobster had discussed Bufalino before, but only as it related to his personal dealings with DeNaples and Sica.

Now, the police needed to hear more. They had a working knowledge of Bufalino, including his reign over the local garment industry, the gambling rackets and rumors of his ties to the Teamsters. But they needed to hear more, especially since, long after his death, his nearly fifty-year legacy continued to influence modern-day events, and they were starting with Big Billy.

# THREE

———

During the latter part of the nineteenth century, thousands of Italian immigrants from Sicily departed their ships in New York Harbor following their long transatlantic crossings and boarded trains for the 130-mile trip northwest to the Wyoming Valley of Pennsylvania.

Tucked away in the northeastern part of the state and separated by the winding Susquehanna River, with the cities of Scranton to the north and Wilkes-Barre to the south, the region was rich in coal and drew new immigrants seeking work in the mines. Nineteenth-century coal mining was brutal. Men worked long hours deep beneath the ground for barely livable wages, with many falling sick, suffering injuries or being killed on a daily basis from a variety of dangers. Paid by the tonnage, the low wages were often given right back to the mine companies to buy food at the company-owned pantries and to rent the shacks in "mining patch" villages that housed the miners and their families.

Before the Italian wave of the late nineteenth century, the accents in many of the villages were Scottish and Irish. But the Sicilians also saw opportunity, with many of them having worked the sulfur mines near their hometown of Montedoro and seeing the promise of living in a new country at the beginning of a new century as an improvement over the few opportunities in Montedoro, which means "mountain of gold." Only there was little gold in the Italian hills, where abusive companies forced workers to ply their trade in extremely dangerous working conditions and used boys as young as ten years old to dig deep into the earth.

Aside from the dangers below, the Montedoro miners had to be just as alert above the surface, given they had little choice but to bend to the will of the local Mafia lords, who were a corrupting presence in nearly every facet of Sicilian society.

Extortion demands were commonplace, and failure to pay the premium often resulted in harassment, and even death. As word spread of the new opportunities afforded in America, particularly for mining in the Wyoming Valley, the Sicilian exodus began.

So across the Atlantic they came, following the Germans and the Irish and the other Europeans, the men and women and children of Montedoro, who settled in the lush valley to work the coal mines, bringing with them their language, food and Old World customs, which unfortunately included the criminal element that plagued them back home.

Giuseppe LaTorre sailed into New York Harbor on the SS *California* in 1902. A member of the Sicilian Mafia, LaTorre was joined a year later by his seventeen-year-old son, Stefano, who despite his youth was also a seasoned member of Montedoro's Mafia and arrived in Pennsylvania experienced in extortion, loan sharking and murder.

Calogero Bufalino, later known as Charles, arrived around the same time with his brother Angelo and cousin Salvatore. Like Stefano LaTorre, Charles Bufalino had built a fearful reputation that followed him to his new home, a reputation topped only by Santo Volpe. At twenty-six, Volpe arrived in 1906 and was Stefano LaTorre's brother-in-law. He had come to Pennsylvania to work the mines and with Bufalino and LaTorre to exploit their fellow immigrant miners.

They quickly made their mark. In 1907, a Philadelphia newspaper published a letter from a Wilkes-Barre resident that told of the problems they faced from the group, who were known throughout the community as the "Black Hand."

*The Black Hand Society has virtually had a free hand in the county. It has systematically levied tribute upon hundreds of Italians who paid considerable sums for protection from violence, and has committed numerous outrages upon others who refused to be blackmailed. The authorities have been almost helpless. Until the advent of the State Constabulary the District Attorney's office had no force to make wholesale arrests, and, besides, fear sealed the mouths of the victims. The fate of informers was well understood, for the society took pains to impress upon its victims that those who have evidence against any member would suffer violent death.*

*On numerous occasions frightened Italians have informed the police that they have received the usual threatening letter signed by the Black Hand, or have been personally threatened; but when told they would be required to appear as witnesses, they wilted, declared they could not identify anyone; that they had had not even a suspicion of who the agents of the society were, and were glad to get away from the authorities and go back to their homes. Many have fled from the region to avoid the wrath of the society. Even in flight there was no safety. A few months ago an Italian who refused tribute fled with his family to Berwick, and there one morning was called to his door by three men and shot dead. There is no clue to his murderers. Another who gave information a year or so ago against the organization was shot dead late at night at Pittston. Again there was no clue. A third was shot, beheaded, and his body thrown into a mine hole near Browntown. There have been scores of outrages. Houses have been dynamited, men have been waylaid and wounded, women have been terrorized, houses have been fired upon or set on fire, but rarely have there been any arrests.*

That changed on April 22, 1907, when Volpe, LaTorre and Charles Bufalino were arrested, along with twenty other men, for terrorizing the mining communities. Among the charges were attempted murder, dynamiting and conspiracy. The issues surrounding the poor treatment of miners in the Wyoming Valley became something of a national issue, and police departments as far away as New York City traveled to Wilkes-Barre to attend the trial, as did agents of the U.S. Secret Service. Witnesses testified that the defendants were part of a vast Italian criminal society with more than five hundred members in cities throughout the northeast, from New York to Buffalo.

One witness, Charles Rizzo, testified that someone placed dynamite at his home after he had refused written demands for $500 payments. Another refusal brought a fuselage of bullets. Rizzo went to the local police, which led to the arrests of Bufalino, LaTorre and Volpe. The police, in turn, were threatened with death if any of the men went to prison. Bufalino and LaTorre were convicted and sentenced to a year in prison. Volpe was acquitted and released. Within weeks, several local residents who initially refused the extortion demands and cooperated with the police were systematically murdered.

By 1910, the three had gained control of all underworld activities in the region, and their influence spread throughout the Italian communities, particularly in a small town called Pittston. Midway between Scranton and Wilkes-Barre, Pittston became the epicenter of the Italian community, where they had sprouted like the spring bulbs along the river.

By 1914, nearly 200,000 miners were living and working in northeast Pennsylvania, with many working for a mining company owned by LaTorre and Volpe. The two men's familiarity with the burgeoning unions, combined with their growing wealth, allowed them to bribe mining union officials, along with local politicians and the police. They also extorted money from other mining companies eager to avoid labor issues. When Prohibition arrived, in 1920, they expanded their operations into bootlegging, and their wealth and power grew tenfold. With even more money to bribe local police, politicians and mining officials, Volpe, LaTorre and Charles Bufalino gained wider influence of local mining operations. Among the men under their control was Frank Agati, a district organizer for the United Mine Workers (UMW) who also was a silent partner with Volpe and LaTorre in their Pennsylvania Coal Company. Agati ensured labor peace for his partners while at the same time served as a bodyguard for his boss, Rinaldo Cappellini, the president of the UMW's District 1.

Toward the end of 1927, Cappellini's leadership, supported by Volpe, LaTorre and Charles Bufalino, was challenged by Alex Campbell, an international union board member who took control of the Pittston-based Local 1703. But just weeks later, Campbell's treasurer was shot and killed as he left a union meeting. Campbell sought to quell the violence and sent three of his men, including Samuel Bonita, president of Local 1703, to Wilkes-Barre to meet with the UMW at its union headquarters. To their surprise, Frank Agati was present. An argument ensued with Bonita, shots were fired and Agati fell dead. Bonita was arrested, and over the next few weeks, several of the reform-minded union leaders were shot and killed, including Campbell, who was returning home with another union official from a meeting with local law enforcement when a car pulled alongside and opened fire with several shotgun blasts.

The violence prompted Pittston mayor William Gillespie to write a letter to UMW president John L. Lewis begging for help to end the bloodshed.

*The hostile factions in the local organization have created a reign of terror by their lawlessness, dynamiting, murder and murder attempts, which are of frequent occurrence. Two prominent leaders of mine workers were murdered in cold blood in the heart of this city last evening. Our city is in a state of terror and turmoil. The cause of this bloody feud or vendetta is known to every intelligent person in the anthracite coal region. This disgraceful and tragic situation is attributed directly to the bitter hostilities that exist between mine officials, mine contractors, union labor leaders and insurgent labor leaders connected with the Pennsylvania Coal Company.*

*The public believes that yourself, district Union President Cappellini and the head of the Pennsylvania Coal Company can end these hostilities and bring this campaign of crime to a close, if you meet together and make an honest effort to settle this deadly dispute.*

Cappellini resigned his position as president of UMW District 1 in June 1928, and his replacement, John Boyland, promised to end the corruption. A year later, the Pennsylvania Coal Company closed. Volpe, LaTorre and Charles Bufalino realized they were unable to control their own local and decided to focus on other business interests, particularly bootlegging, which was far more profitable. Other issues had also led to their dissolution, including LaTorre's refusal to pay his share of the payment made to the murderers of Campbell and the other union representatives.

Despite the division within their own ranks, the men were resolved to exact revenge for the loss of their coal interests. They waited a few years, but in 1931, bodies again filled the streets of Pittston. One man, Calogero Calamera, a UMW official who had sided with Campbell, was shot six times. Police arrested two men in the Calamera murder, including Joseph Barbara. A petty criminal and bootlegger, Barbara was an assassin for the Buffalo crime family run by Stefano Magaddino before moving to Kingston in the late 1920s. He was released from custody after police determined they didn't have enough evidence to hold him. Two years later, in 1933, Barbara was arrested again, this time for the murder of Sam Wichner, a bootlegger who snatched a whiskey shipment owned by Volpe, who had become the recognized leader of the Pittston mob.

Barbara, who by now lived in Endicott, New York, just west of Binghamton on New York's southern tier, near the

Pennsylvania border, had summoned Wichner to his home for a meeting. Wichner left that meeting alive but was told to come back for another sit-down the following night. Wichner's body was found a week later with a noose around his neck in the back of a car in Scranton. Again, with little evidence, Barbara escaped prosecution.

But his stock grew in 1932 following Volpe's arrest in New York for his alleged role in the murder of John Bazzano, the Mafia boss of Pittsburgh. Bazzano had ordered the execution of three fellow Pittsburgh gangsters, who happened to have had ties to Vito Genovese, the leader of one of the five families in New York. Bazzano was summoned to Brooklyn to answer for the murders, and his body was later found in a sack infiltrated with numerous cuts from an ice pick. More than a dozen men were arrested, including Volpe, but they were later released due to lack of evidence.

The incident, and the arrest, spooked Volpe, and he decided to step down as the leader of the Pittston mob. In his midfifties, Volpe was wealthy and had interests in numerous legitimate businesses. In his place, to run the Pittston mob, Volpe named John Sciandra.

A former miner who became a mob Everyman under Volpe and one of his most trusted lieutenants, Sciandra assumed control following the end of Prohibition, in 1933. The coal industry was in a tailspin as oil was fast becoming the dominate energy supplier, which resulted in less and less demand for coal. But another industry had given rise in the Wyoming Valley, and instead of meeting the nation's energy needs, the region was fast becoming a dominant player in the garment industry, where immigrants again toiled for pennies in nonunion shops. By 1937, Sciandra needed help with the growing industry, and he summoned his brother-in-law.

# Four

───────

Rosario Bufalino—Charles Bufalino's nephew—was two months old when he arrived in America in 1904. His family had followed hundreds of other immigrants from Montedoro, Sicily, over the vast ocean to the new country, and after settling in Manhattan for a few months, the new immigrants followed a well-traveled road for Italians out of New York that took them upstate to Buffalo.

After his mother, Cristina, died in 1910, Rosario returned to Sicily with his older brother Giuseppe but returned to Buffalo in 1914. By the time he was a teenager, young Rosario was known by his American name, Russell, and he learned a trade as an automobile mechanic. But his real work was pursuing some of the Old World customs, such as petty thefts, selling stolen property, hijacking and other assorted crimes. Deemed smart, resourceful and, most important, trustworthy, Russell had grown into a young man when he caught the attention of John Montana, the underboss for the Buffalo crime family's head, Stefano Magaddino.

Magaddino was also Sicilian but hailed from Castellammare del Golfo, a northwestern coastal village. Born in 1891, Magaddino followed his father Giovanni's footsteps into the Sicilian Mafia but fled the island after an older brother was killed. He originally settled in Brooklyn with a cousin, Vito Bonaventure, who headed a group of paid killers that took Magaddino under their wing. Within a short time, Magaddino was linked to several murders in New York and was subsequently charged with killing a New Jersey man. He was later released when a witness recanted. After escaping an assassination attempt, Magaddino fled to Buffalo to work under Giuseppe DiCarlo. When DiCarlo died, in 1922, Magaddino quickly assumed control of the family. Though illiterate, Magaddino amassed a fortune due chiefly to the burgeoning liquor trade that grew during Prohibition. Magaddino's strength was the ports he controlled on Lake Erie, from which he allowed other crime families from other cities, such as Cleveland and New York, to smuggle alcohol from Canada. Of course, he took a percentage of each shipment.

By 1930, Magaddino's crime syndicate bore his name, and his vast wealth and ruthlessness earned him the respect and stature as one of the most powerful organized crime leaders in the United States. In addition to his illegal ventures, Magaddino also had a number of legitimate businesses, including ownership of several funeral parlors, which earned him the nickname "the Undertaker." An astute businessman, Magaddino conducted his business privately, quietly and, when necessary, violently. In 1931, Magaddino's stature in Italian organized crime circles reached its zenith when he was given a seat on the newly formed Commission, the appointed national leadership of *La Cosa Nostra*.

A bloody war between two New York Castellammare families that had torn the Italian mob apart was ended when several young, up-and-coming gangsters, led by Charles "Lucky" Luciano, assassinated the leaders. To preserve future peace, Luciano and several others scheduled a meeting in Chicago with the purpose of establishing a governing body that would settle disputes between the various mob families. The heads of New York's five families were appointed to the new board, along with Al Capone, from Chicago, and Magaddino, from Buffalo, with Luciano serving as the Commission's first chairman. The group agreed to meet every few years or as needed when called on to iron out differences among warring mob families with the understanding that the Commission would be the final authority.

Throughout the 1920s, Bufalino watched and learned from the powerful Magaddino, and his rising profile and stature within the family drew Magaddino's respect. He didn't hesitate, for instance, to call upon his young protégé to snuff out enemies, a familiar task for anyone who sought to become a "made" member of the family, that is, to be officially inducted into the organized crime family.

There would also be several arrests. Bufalino was

charged by the Buffalo police in 1927 and again in 1935 for receiving stolen property. At five feet eight inches and only 138 pounds, Bufalino wasn't an imposing figure. He had black hair and dull, gray eyes, with a three-inch vaccination scar above his elbow and an L-shaped scar above the right temple. His left eyelid drooped, the result of a muscle irregularity in his face, and it gave him a somewhat comic appearance. But Bufalino had a steely resolve and intelligence that set him apart from the other young hoods, and he became an important underworld figure in Buffalo and one of Magaddino's trusted lieutenants. Bufalino was so highly thought of, he was guided to take a bride from another important Sicilian family, this one from northeastern Pennsylvania.

In 1928, Bufalino married Caroline Sciandra. Her family had emigrated in the late 1800s from Montedoro, following the road from New York to the Wyoming Valley. Her brother, John, was a miner whose real work involved extortion, loan sharking and murder under the direction of Santo Volpe. The marriage unified the Sciandra and Bufalino families, which had family members living in Buffalo and the Scranton area. It also came with the blessing of Magaddino, who soon after sent another rising hood, Joseph Barbara, to northeastern Pennsylvania to watch over Magaddino's bootlegging interests.

Barbara was a young man with a temper who'd so much as stick a knife in you as he would shake your hand, and it wasn't long after his arrival in 1930 from Buffalo that he was linked to the murder of a Magaddino rival. The charges were later dropped, but Barbara remained in the region and was tasked with a variety of jobs, including contract killings. At times when he needed help, Russell Bufalino was dispatched to assist him.

Barbara eventually moved north, just over the Pennsylvania–New York border to Endicott, New York, where he opened a soft-drink distribution plant. In 1938, Russell Bufalino and his wife, Carla, moved to Pennsylvania. Bufalino's marriage to a Sciandra, along with his blood relation to his uncle Charles Bufalino, made him the perfect choice to assist John Sciandra, who took over control of all organized crime activity from Santo Volpe, who decided to "retire" after beating back a murder charge in 1933. Russell was now firmly entrenched as his brother-in-law's underboss.

For legitimacy purposes, Bufalino was employed as an auto mechanic at the Canada Dry bottling plant owned by Barbara, though it was nothing more than a ruse to cover his real work, which, by the end of World War II, focused on union racketeering and the garment industry.

BY 1945, THE thousands of women who worked in the Wyoming Valley's nonunion garment manufacturing centers were earning as little as $16 per week.

With most of their coal-miner husbands returning from the war but unable to find work, the women had no choice but to submit to the demands of the garment plants, where they often labored twelve to sixteen hours per day. Little girls as young as ten years old could also be found stitching the individual pieces produced at the plants. To the bosses, it didn't matter how old the workers were, as long as the work got done. They were modern-day sweatshops, and there were dozens throughout the region, from Scranton through Pittston to Wilkes-Barre and Hazleton. Because of the low pay and awful working conditions, the industry did little to stimulate the economic rebirth of a region still struggling with the demise of coal.

Yet throughout the Wyoming Valley, especially in and around Pittston, many of the dress factories that lined the main street were owned by Russell Bufalino.

The New York City–based garment industry relied on northeastern Pennsylvania as a source of cheap labor at a time when the industry's major union, the International Ladies' Garment Workers Union (ILGWU), was making headway unionizing New York's shops. For decades, organizers with the ILGWU fought for and eventually gained a major foothold among garment workers in New York City. It wasn't easy. Cracked skulls, broken bones, gunshot wounds and even death awaited many of the organizers from Mafiosi eager to keep their costs low and profits high.

Undeterred, the ILGWU eventually forced many of the organized crime–owned garment firms to seek cheaper labor elsewhere. And it didn't come any cheaper, or under more control, than in northeast Pennsylvania.

The region's close proximity to New York and the dire economy created a perfect storm of conditions. Any work was better than no work, and many of the shops, initially fueled by Magaddino money from Buffalo, were highly profitable and earned more than enough to pay the bribes required by the local police chiefs, politicians, and local and county officials, who all turned a blind eye to complaints.

With nowhere to turn, the few who would confront the industry were usually met with stiff resistance through threats, violence, bombed homes and even murder. Among those consulting Russell Bufalino were his uncle Charles and Santo Volpe, and their experiences dating back to the violence used against the mining communities served as a valuable lesson plan.

By the early 1940s, Russell had ownership stakes in at least a dozen garment businesses, including the Pennsylvania Drape and Curtain Company, Ann Lee Frocks Company and Alamo Dress Manufacturing Company, all in Pittston, and Dixie Frocks Company, in Wyoming, Pennsylvania. The garments made in those shops would be shipped, usually by truck, to New York, where they'd be sold by jobbers to large, national department-store chains. At the end of World War II, the garment industry had supplanted coal as one of organized crime's chief businesses, and Russell Bufalino was becoming a major force within mob circles.

# FIVE

The dinner given in honor of Vito Genovese upon his return to America in 1945 was one fit for a king.

Genovese was among the young, extremely violent hoods who, along with Frank Costello and Albert Anastasia, helped Lucky Luciano in his climb to the top of the Commission in 1931. It was Genovese who conspired with Luciano to plot the murders of Giuseppe "Joseph" Masseria, then the "boss of bosses," and Salvatore Maranzano. Their demise paved the way for the new organization that would dictate future business and settle disputes.

Born in 1897 near Naples, Genovese had a propensity for violence that often left a trail of bodies, including the love interests of women Genovese courted. He was also an ambitious businessman working for Masseria who earned his keep via bootlegging and extortion. Genovese's business interests in the 1920s led to his introduction to

Russell Bufalino and the Magaddino family. The two men shared more than their Italian heritage—both were rising through the ranks of their respective crime families.

Named by Luciano as the leader of one of New York's five crime families, Genovese was elevated in 1936 to temporarily replace Luciano as head of the Commission after Luciano was convicted for pandering. But Genovese had his own legal problems, having been indicted in a 1934 murder. Fearing imprisonment, Genovese fled to Italy, where he settled and became an early supporter of dictator Benito Mussolini.

That changed in 1944. With the outcome of the war certain, Genovese began working for the Allies as an interpreter. And when he wasn't helping U.S. forces, Genovese was earning thousands in the black market selling food and supplies stolen from U.S. Army trucks. He was subsequently arrested by the Military Police but never tried. When the war ended, he was returned to Brooklyn to stand trial for the 1934 murder, but the key witness in the case had died after mysteriously taking medication laced with poison.

Upon Genovese's release, he was feted at a welcome-home dinner in New York attended by top Mafiosi, among them his old friend Russell Bufalino. But the dynamics of the New York crime families had changed, and another old friend, Frank Costello, was now in charge. Costello was born in Calabria, Italy, in 1891 and like thousands of other Italian immigrants arrived by ship into New York Harbor in 1900. He joined a gang as a teen and had several brushes with the law for robbery and petty crimes. By

1920, he counted Luciano and Genovese as friends and business partners. Their business interests swelled with Prohibition, and the young gangsters expanded into other underworld pursuits, including gambling, prostitution and bookmaking.

While Luciano and Genovese provided the muscle for the triumvirate, Costello made alliances with local politicians, judges and key law enforcement officials, providing them with thousands of dollars in payoffs. As Luciano rose to the head of the new Commission, Genovese and Costello were given titles of underboss and consigliere, respectively. Another member of their group, Albert Anastasia, was awarded with a leadership role in the infamous "Murder Incorporated," the group that carried out dozens of mob executions for the Commission.

But Genovese's departure to Italy opened the door for Costello's ascent, and his cerebral management style and political contacts proved lucrative. By 1945, Costello's position as boss could not be challenged, not even by Genovese, who quietly seethed but decided to bide his time. There was, after all, business to conduct.

By the end of the war, the New York mob bosses had major financial interests in the garment industry, Costello and Anastasia included. And those interests included ownership of nonunion manufacturing shops in Pennsylvania. From the end of the 1930s through World War II, the mob lords reaped their garment industry profits in relative peace with little to fear from law enforcement or anyone else, for that matter, thanks chiefly to their strongest partner, Russell Bufalino.

By 1945, Costello and Anastasia had established strong alliances with Bufalino, who himself had varied interests in their home turf of New York City. Bufalino spent a lot of time in New York, arriving in Manhattan on a Monday and staying through Wednesday. He had a suite at the Hotel Forrester in midtown and would conduct business at a restaurant he owned, the Vesuvio, in midtown on West Forty-Eighth Street.

Along with the restaurant, Bufalino owned or was a part owner of several dress shops in the garment industry and jewelry shops along Manhattan's famed "Diamond District" on West Forty-Seventh Street. An astute jeweler, Bufalino always carried a magnifying glass to look at newly stolen loads of diamonds, gold, rubies and other precious stones that had been taken from someone's house, a store or right off the body of a lifeless victim. Back home in Pennsylvania, Bufalino operated his wide-ranging interests, particularly those in the garment industry, with little interference from law enforcement nor any of the burgeoning unions.

And then came Min Matheson.

A representative from the International Ladies' Garment Workers Union (ILGWU), Matheson arrived in Wilkes-Barre in 1945 with one mission: to unionize the thousands of poorly paid, overworked women who labored in garment shops like those owned by Bufalino.

Prior to Matheson's arrival, only a handful of shops were aligned with the ILGWU, and her sudden arrival in Pittston, Bufalino's home turf, didn't go unnoticed. In 1946, Matheson convinced some thirty sewing-machine operators to picket in front of a Bufalino dress shop on Pittston's Main Street. Matheson led the picket line but was treated to an onslaught of insults from some of the locals who gathered to watch. Some of Bufalino's men were there, holding bats and waving shotguns while menacing the women. But Matheson and her strikers continued to picket the shop, and they remained there day after day for eight months. They were the first salvos in a war that would last years.

Bufalino responded in 1946 by organizing his own union, the Anthracite Needle Workers Association. Membership in Bufalino's union was small but increased incrementally when workers pressed by Bufalino's men were quietly reminded that just a few years earlier it was Bufalino who was behind the damage at the Lori Dress Company, where two hundred sewing machines were destroyed in a bid to put Lori Dress out of business.

Bufalino was never charged, but everyone knew, including law enforcement, who was behind it. Undeterred by Bufalino or his threats, Matheson was relentless, visiting dress and manufacturing shops throughout the region and slowly convincing women to take the leap and unionize.

By 1949, Matheson's efforts were bearing fruit. She had union contracts with more than forty dress factories, and her war with Bufalino was now affecting the profit margins of other organized crime leaders who had interests in the Pennsylvania garment industry, among them Albert Anastasia.

Anastasia's interests in the garment industry included

stores in New York and factories in Pennsylvania. When Matheson began organizing a nonunion shop near Hazleton owned by Anastasia, his unhappiness with the situation was made clear to Bufalino. The resulting solution involved Matheson's brother, Will Lurye. A father of four children, Lurye joined his sister as union organizer, giving up a $150-per-week job as a presser to follow the family calling for union organizing for $80 per week.

While Matheson was picketing Anastasia's Hazleton shop, Lurye was marching in New York in front of another manufacturing plant connected to Anastasia. But just days after setting up the picket line, Lurye was accosted by two men inside a public telephone booth and stabbed repeatedly. He died within minutes.

Lurye's murder was front-page news in New York, but its real purpose was to serve as a clear message to Matheson in Pennsylvania. Her father, who was in the hospital when her brother was killed, died a week later. He too had been a union organizer and instilled the same spirit and belief in his children. Instead of packing and leaving, Matheson instead was emboldened by her brother's murder, and she subsequently focused her unionizing efforts on Pittston's Main Street, which was Bufalino's home turf.

Matheson specifically picketed one garment manufacturer that had joined another Bufalino-led union, the Northeastern Pennsylvania Needle Worker's Association, which was run by Bufalino's brother-in-law, Angelo Sciandra. Their slogan was "Sign with us, or you'll be sorry." Some worried workers signed, while others held out. The racketeers union infuriated Matheson, who continued to visit Pittston daily despite warnings from her superiors in New York to stay away. As the threats continued, Matheson persisted. One night, while walking in Pittston, Matheson was approached from behind by a man who pleaded with her to get out of town.

"For God's sake, Min. They've ordered me to close my shop. They've threatened my family," he said.

The plea had the opposite effect on Matheson, who went public with her crusade. She gave interviews to newspapers and, in one radio appearance, told the host that "to live by permission of goons is worse than death. Gentlemen, hoodlums, I don't scare easily."

And she didn't. Each year, Matheson made gains, and one by one, the nonunion, gangster-controlled shops were slowly brought into the ILGWU's fold. By 1953, Matheson had unionized sixty new shops and seven hundred employees. The numbers were still somewhat small when judged against the hundreds of small shops that operated throughout the region, but the growth continued to attract Bufalino's attention. By 1955, for instance, for every new shop that Matheson brought into the ILGWU, Bufalino would send her a funeral-sized floral arrangement, while intimidation and violence were never far away. During one potentially explosive march in front of a Bufalino-owned shop, Matheson and her picketers were serenaded with catcalls and pleas from Bufalino's associates to bring their husbands with them. Irate, Matheson saw Bufalino watching from across the street as his men cursed the female picketers, and she broke ranks and walked toward him. Standing only five feet three inches, Matheson lashed out, "I don't need my husband to protect me. I'm twice the man you'll ever be, Russ Bufalino."

Bufalino didn't reply, and after a long pause, the women on the picket line cheered as Matheson returned to join them.

The decade-long battle with Min Matheson led to several investigations of New York's garment industry. Law enforcement for years had tried to get its hands around the mob-controlled shops, and state and federal law agencies impaneled investigative grand juries to probe the industry in attempts to flush out organized crime influence in the garment industry and labor racketeering, though with little success.

In 1950, the U.S. government also decided to take a closer look, and the Senate Special Committee to Investigate Crime in Interstate Commerce was formed. Headed by chairman Senator Estes Kefauver, the committee eventually expanded its focus and probed the mob's influence in several industries.

The Kefauver Committee, as it was known, held more than a dozen hearings, and for the very first time, the U.S. public had an opportunity to take a peek inside organized crime. The FBI, under J. Edgar Hoover, had put his resources into fighting Communism and had long dismissed the notion that a national Italian crime syndicate even existed. But the committee found there was in fact an organized crime structure that was, in many places, aided and abetted by law enforcement, which cared little about the mobsters' activities so long as they remained out of sight and produced little violence.

"The public knows that the tentacles of organized crime reach into virtually every community throughout the country. It also knows that law enforcement is essentially a local matter calling for constant vigilance at the local level and a strengthening of public and private morality," read a passage from the report.

The committee put a particular focus on law enforcement and wanted to know why police throughout the country seemingly looked the other way when it came to lucrative vices, such as gambling. One of the cities studied was Scranton, where by 1950, Bufalino held a death grip not just over the garment industry, but over all gambling activity in Scranton and the Wyoming Valley. No poker parlor or sports book could operate without Bufalino's permission, and he collected a cut of all gross profits while the police looked the other way.

In its final report, in 1951, the committee delivered a lengthy and scathing criticism of Scranton law enforcement and police departments in neighboring cities and towns:

> *Gambling Law-enforcement officials in Scranton seemingly are afflicted with the same peculiar blindness toward organized gambling that has been apparent to the committee in its inquiries in other cities. Four horse rooms running wide open and heavily patronized were found by committee investigators. A numbers banker*

*testified that he did business for twenty years without ever having been arrested himself, although there were three or four occasions when his runners were picked up. Punchboards littered store counters, and U.S. Treasury balance tickets were openly sold. It is clearly evident that there is a strange reluctance on the part of the police in Scranton to arrest anybody for violations of the gambling laws. Horse rooms are never raided. Periodically, when "the heat is on," the order goes out to "close and stay closed," but such an edict lacks any prolonged or lasting effectiveness. The same can also be said for the cities of Pittston and Wilkes-Barre adjoining Luzerne County.*

*To units of the Pennsylvania State Police must go credit for the only successful forays against the gambling interests, even though they usually follow a policy of not going into the cities unless requested to do so by the district attorney or city officials themselves.*

*In March of this year, without notice to the Scranton police, several details of state police staged a series of raids in the city designed to cripple the operations of Louis Cohen. Vast quantities of Treasury-balance tickets, printing equipment, engraving plates, stapling machines and supplies were seized. Seven persons were arrested. The value of the seized material was in excess of $50,000, and the tickets being processed were intended for distribution in the months between October 1951 and February 1952. A similar seizure in Wilkes-Barre, also by the state police, yielded an even greater volume of tickets, materials and equipment, and struck hard at the source of supply for so-called independent operators not* linked with Cohen. The committee endeavored unsuccessfully to serve a subpoena on Cohen prior to its hearing in Washington on August 7 in connection with the Scranton investigation. Accompanied by counsel, Cohen subsequently appeared in Washington and presented himself to the committee, but insufficient time remained for proper interrogation of the witness.

While Cohen was evading process, the committee subpoenaed his chief lieutenant in Pennsylvania, Patrick Joseph Size, of Scranton. Claiming that his answers would tend to incriminate him, Size refused to give any testimony about his activities or his dealings with Cohen. He also refused to explain suspicious long-distance telephone calls made every Friday from his home to Allentown, Reading, Schuylkill Haven, Wilkes-Barre and Williamsport.

Jimmy Mack, of Wilkes-Barre, also known as Vincenzo Maccarone, testified before the committee. He admitted owning pinball machines and a few slot machines and said that he grossed $50 to $60 a day as a numbers banker in Wilkes-Barre. Pretending that he did not know whether the numbers business was against the law, he pointed to the fact that the police never interfered with him or gave him trouble in connection with his slot machines. He added that he operated the slot machines in private clubs outside the city, and none of them ever was seized.

Captain Harry E. McElroy, director of the Bureau of Criminal Identification and Information of the Pennsylvania State Police, with headquarters at Harrisburg, told the committee that Sergeant Charles Hartman, of the state police, had reported a bribe offer from Jimmy Mack, acting on behalf of Cohen, and that the state police commissioner had given instructions to Hartman "to string Mack along," because all signs indicated that the time was approaching to close in on the Cohen operations. The advisability of trying to bait Cohen into passing the bribe was considered, but this was eventually abandoned in favor of the direct thrust that would cripple his operations. Mack denied the bribe offer, but the committee sees no reason for doubting the word of Captain McElroy.

The Treasury-balance racket, Captain McElroy said, has two divisions. In one division are a number of independent operators. The other division consists of the syndicate headed by Cohen. The state is divided into districts with separate organizations in each district. The racket runs into many millions; in fact, Captain McElroy estimated that it grosses more than $30 million per year, with the syndicate operation accounting for more than $20 million of this figure. He identified Size as Cohen's principal representative in Pennsylvania and declared that information in the hands of the state police indicates that Cohen operates on an interstate basis.

Captain McElroy told the committee that raids made during the past one and one-half years have resulted in confiscation of millions of tickets and printing equipment, material and supplies worth tremendous amounts of money, but he complained that it is difficult to get evidence against the leaders. "They sit behind somewhere and the money comes in to them and they don't have direct operations, and that's that," Captain McElroy declared. He estimated that the operators realize net profit of about 20 percent of the gross intake. He said he had heard of many instances where the racket interests refused to pay the big "hits."

Captain McElroy was asked whether use of the U.S. Treasury balance has the psychological effect of giving the lottery the benefit of the prestige of the federal government. He testified that he was certain that this was so.

George T. Harris, superintendent of the Washington office of Western Union, testified that a Western Union employee is sent every morning to obtain the Treasury balance, and he transmits it directly from the Treasury Department to Western Union's commercial news department in New York. The number is wired from there to Chicago, from which it is wired to sixteen subscribers to this special service. Fifty-one subscribers in the East are serviced from New York. Three Scranton subscribers are included in the list.

The committee also questioned Joseph Baldassari, a partner in the Baldassari Amusement Company, but he proved to be extremely uncooperative. The committee had information to the effect that Baldassari and his brother Al are engaged in an extensive gambling enterprise operating under official sanction. However, he refused to answer most of the questions put to him on the ground that his answer might tend to incriminate him. He produced voluminous records but refused to disclose their contents. He refused to say whether he knew Louis Cohen and other underworld characters or whether he took Scranton police on trips in his airplane. He did admit, however, that his father was Ulisses Baldassari, who furnished the bail for the seven defendants arrested by the state police in the raids on Cohen's printing operations.

He declined to say whether he owned any slot machines and whether his brother ran a horse room at 108 Adams Avenue. He also refused to say whether he had paid protection money to any official or whether it was true that he had given a $2,500 ring to the director of public safety.

At first he refused to name the partners in Baldassari Amusement Company, but he was finally compelled to admit that they consisted of himself, his brother Al and their two wives. He was unwilling to try to reconcile this with the fact that the firm's income-tax returns listed only the two wives as the partners.

The district attorney of Lackawanna County, Carlon M. O'Malley, gave what seemed to the committee to be a rather unsatisfactory explanation of the small number of gambling prosecutions in his county. He said his office by tradition is a prosecuting office, not a policing agency, although he does have four county detectives. He said he would be naive if he attempted to tell the committee that the Scranton horse rooms did not exist or had not existed for a number of years, but he claimed that the responsibility for any laxity rested with the city police department, which has 175 uniformed men and 12 detectives. He referred to the state police raids on the Cohen lottery ticket printing establishment last March, in connection with which Patrick Joseph Size, Gregory Size, and others received fines ranging from $200 to $300, but no jail sentences were imposed.

O'Malley stated that on June 29, while on vacation, he issued orders to his staff to conduct a survey of gambling in the areas of Lackawanna County outside of Scranton. This was prompted, he said, by the reappearance of Cohen-controlled Treasury-balance lottery tickets in the county. It is significant to note that this committee's investigators entered Scranton on June 20, and their presence was publicly announced several days before Mr. O'Malley ordered his survey.

He said his staff reported back that they and the state police had communicated with all police chiefs in the communities outside of Scranton and had been informed that they had no knowledge of gambling, with the exception of punchboards, which they promised to suppress forthwith.

Mr. O'Malley submitted to the committee a report of the survey, which showed that warnings to cease operations had been given to all suspected gamblers, including Louis Cohen, although Cohen's chief lieutenant, Patrick Joseph Size, was not in Scranton when the warning was issued. In spite of Mr. O'Malley's disclaimer of responsibility for gambling in the city of Scranton, the "close and stay closed" order described in his report was issued to a number of Scranton gamblers.

Committee counsel posed this question to Mr. O'Malley: "I wonder if you can explain why it is the place stays wide open until our investigators arrive and our *investigators can find it [gambling] like any other citizen, yet the police are not doing anything about it. Are the police receiving protection for that?" His answer was, "I have no knowledge of that and cannot answer it." Mr. O'Malley's attention was also called to the fact that the horse room in the Greyhound Terminal Building was across the street from the district attorney's office, and the Baldassari horse room was in the next block. He acknowledged that a gambling place in Carbondale was located in a building owned by the mother of the prothonotary of Lackawanna County.*

*Mr. O'Malley argued that crime conditions in Lackawanna County are far better than they were prior to World War II. He attributed this improvement largely to the action of the U.S. Army and the FBI.*

*Joseph Scalleat, a Hazleton racketeer, was recommended for contempt by the committee after a brief but highly irritating appearance. He refused to bring records as directed by the subpoena because he "didn't think it was necessary," and he defiantly told the committee at the outset that he was going to refuse to answer all questions. He refused to tell the committee what business he was pursuing, whether he had any brothers named Sam and Albert, or if he knew Jack Parisi, a former New York convict, or had any contacts with him. He refused to say if he remembered Parisi's arrest by state police in a hideout located in a building occupied by his sister and her husband.*

*David F. Haggerty, a constable in Scranton for twelve years and an owner of harness-racing horses, re-*

fused to tell the committee whether he had any interest in the horse room on Penn Avenue operated by James "Buz" Caffrey. He admitted that he gave no attention to his duties as constable because it was strictly a commission or fee office, and "I just never went in for it." He testified that he derives no income from being a constable and that he "just about breaks even" in the operation of his stable, but he declined to answer when questioned about the source of $19,500 in "commissions" listed in his income-tax returns for 1949 and 1950.

The committee asked Mr. Haggerty, "Do you know of any political contributions made from the gambling interests in connection with the political life of Scranton?" His answer was, "I will have to decline to answer that on the grounds it may tend to incriminate me."

Thomas Sesso, who has lived in Scranton thirty-three years, has been a numbers banker for twenty years and has never been arrested himself, although his runners were apprehended three or four times. He told the committee he grossed $15,000 to $20,000 a year and operated only in a couple of blocks in the central city because "when a man don't stretch too far the police never get you."

There were times during his years as a numbers banker that he was compelled to suspend operations. How did he know "when the heat was on"? His answer: "The city gives the order out to the cops, something comes out, then I just stop." As a numbers banker, he has done well financially. When he gave up his shoemaking establishment twenty years ago, he had nothing. Now he has

$20,000, in cash, three properties, money invested in a mortgage and a Lincoln automobile. He was asked, "You are retiring now on your earnings?" He replied, "That's right. Right now I don't know nothing. When the future coming, I don't know what I do."

Two Scranton police captains appearing before the committee blandly insisted that their manifold duties in other fields of police work left them with little time to enforce gambling laws. Richard Beynon, the day captain, maintained that he was responsible only for traffic control. He knew the horse rooms were operating but didn't know if they had wire service. He knew Treasury tickets were sold in the city, but he claimed he never personally witnessed any sales. He didn't know the Cohens or anything about them, but he knew the Baldassari brothers as "businessmen," and he also knew that the numbers lottery was operating. He did not know of any numbers takers other than Sesso, but he did not think there were any.

The only slot machines Beynon knew anything about were located in veterans' posts and private clubs, but he had no knowledge about whether they were operating. Asked about a raid on a gambling house in West Scranton in which the raiding detail seized eight or nine men but "lost" all but two of them before the arrival of the lieutenant, Beynon said he didn't know whether any disciplinary action had been taken on account of the "loss" of prisoners because that was not under his jurisdiction.

James G. Conaboy, captain on the 4 P.M. to midnight shift, testified he knew very little about the numbers busi-

*ness because operations were virtually over before his shift began. Office details and handling of complaints about disorderly conduct, mischievous boys, etc., keep him so busy "that I do not have the time to personally go out and observe every activity in the city or under my jurisdiction. From the fact that no patrolman, sergeant, or lieutenant has ever submitted verbally or written any complaint to me, I had presumed that the conditions in Scranton were at least favorable, and I had no occasion to suspect anything else."*

*If any gambling violation had been brought to his attention, Conaboy said, he would have made out a report to the superintendent of police, but "I never had a complaint from a subordinate, citizen, or anybody else as to the activities of a horse room or numbers, and therefore I would have no occasion or necessity to submit a report to my superior."*

*The Scranton, Pittston and Wilkes-Barre horse rooms were all "drops" for wire service being supplied by Metro-Globe News Service, of Hoboken, New Jersey. In Scranton, only one operator applied for the service under his own name. The other three adopted the obviously fictitious names of the "Greek Social Club," the "Modern Amusement Co." and the "B. & B. Club." The Pittston subscribers were the "Pittston Social Club" and the "Wyoming Valley Social Club." In Wilkes-Barre, the service was furnished to J. Sheerin.*

*The committee sought the testimony of Jack Parisi, longtime associate of Albert Anastasia, reputed head of Murder, Inc., in New York, about his activities in Ha-*

*zleton, Pennsylvania, but Parisi entered a Philadelphia hospital the day before the committee's hearing in August. Doctors confirmed that he was suffering from a chronic leg injury directly attributed to a bullet wound in the hip sustained many years ago. Parisi vanished from New York in 1939, when police began hunting him for two murders. For ten years he enjoyed sanctuary in Pennsylvania coal-field communities until state police flushed him out of a specially designed hideout in Hazleton and turned him over to the New York authorities. Parisi "beat the rap" in the two murder cases and returned to Hazleton, where he blossomed out as production manager in the Nuremberg Dress Company factory at Nuremberg, a few miles from Hazleton. The owner of the company is Harry Strasser, alias Cohen, alias Lefty, with a New York criminal record. Strasser and Anastasia are partners in the Madison Dress Company in Hazleton, and Strasser is also listed as the owner of the Mount Carmel Garment Company, in Mount Carmel, Pennsylvania; the Bobby Dress Company, in Dickson City, Pennsylvania; and the Interstate Dress Transportation Company. The committee also has evidence of additional infiltration of the garment industry in Pennsylvania by racket interests, but lack of time and funds compelled the committee to forego a more intensive investigation of this phase of racketeering activity in legitimate business.*

*Except for the aggressive investigative accomplishments of the Pennsylvania State Police and their note-*

*worthy efforts to cripple lottery operations centered in the cities of northeastern Pennsylvania, the committee finds that official lethargy toward organized gambling is so appalling as to be shocking to the public conscience.*

*The slap-on-the-wrist attitude evidenced by the "close and stay closed" orders of nebulous tenure can hardly be regarded as an adequate substitute for rigid enforcement that is marked by arrest and conviction and, where the circumstances warrant it, imprisonment.*

# SIX

---

By the middle of 2006, construction had already begun on the new Mount Airy Casino Resort as contractors, engineers and planners zipped through local and county zoning hearings.

After buying the old resort, Louis DeNaples sold off its contents and then proceeded to tear down every building standing. Rising in their place would be a lavish hotel and casino to be accompanied by a retail center and eighteen-hole golf course.

But the plan was modest compared to the larger casino proposed for nearby Pocono Manor. Like Mount Airy, Pocono Manor had a long history as a resort destination, having been owned by the Ireland family for years before they decided to sell to a group led by New Jersey developer Greg Matzel and his silent partner, Morris Bailey, a billionaire conservative Jew who belonged to one of the wealthiest congregations in Brooklyn.

Bailey's money fueled an ambitious plan that would see a new eighteen-story resort hotel rise atop the mountain, complemented by a convention center, an 8,000-seat sports arena, a large lake surrounded by a shopping area and two golf courses. Situated near I-80 and just off I-380, Pocono Manor offered by far the better plan of the two Pocono applicants, and it had a respected industry executive as its president, Dennis Gomes.

Gomes was a major figure in casino circles who in a previous life was a former investigator with the Nevada Gaming Commission who had rooted out much of the organized crime influence in Las Vegas in the late 1970s. Gomes' work was the basis for the Martin Scorsese film *Casino*. Gomes later went on to become the president of several casinos, including the Tropicana and Taj Mahal in Atlantic City, and the Golden Nugget in Las Vegas. His participation in the Pocono Manor project added instant credibility to the plan.

A third application, from Dr. Joseph Mattioli, the owner of famed NASCAR track Pocono Raceway, envisioned a casino placed next door to the tri-oval track. But Mattioli pulled the plan after learning that DeNaples indeed had his eyes set on a gaming license. Mattioli knew that neither he nor Pocono Manor would ever get a license over Louis DeNaples.

The gaming board was on a strict timeline and was looking to award its large, stand-alone gaming licenses by

December 2006. Over the course of that summer, the board began its background investigations, which included assembling all personal and financial records of Louis DeNaples.

Raised in Dunmore, Pennsylvania, DeNaples was born to Margaret, a homemaker, and Patrick, who worked for the Erie-Lackawanna Railroad but made little money, and the story that eventually accompanied any DeNaples biography was that he and his siblings were so poor they received the same sled each year for Christmas while wearing rags on their feet instead of shoes, to the amusement of other children. With no more than an eighth-grade education, DeNaples eventually opened his first junkyard in the 1960s.

As his business grew, DeNaples began to make political contributions to both Democrats and Republicans. By 1969, DeNaples branched out and opened his first landfill in Dunmore after winning the city of Scranton's garbage contract. In 1972, he was named a director of the First National Community Bank, and between his many businesses, DeNaples saw his wealth and stature gradually grow, and some speculated his success was due in part to his relationship with Russell Bufalino.

It was common knowledge that no one could operate anywhere in the region as DeNaples had without Bufalino's blessing, or his cooperation. According to the Pennsylvania Crime Commission, one of Bufalino's top lieutenants, Casper "Cappy" Giumento, was a regular visitor to DeNaples' auto parts store and the landfill, and was believed to be serving as a go-between, passing messages between Bufalino and DeNaples.

A rising power within the state and local community, DeNaples ascent was derailed in 1977 when he was charged with falsifying documents to obtain more than $525,000 in federal reimbursements and was tried with three other men for falsely billing the federal government for cleanup work related to 1972's Hurricane Agnes. DeNaples had rented equipment to Lackawanna County to help with cleanup from the damage caused by the devastating hurricane, and the county timekeeper, Louis Coviello Sr., fixed the books by crediting more work time for the equipment. The county investigated and found the discrepancies, and DeNaples, Coviello and two others were charged with fraud. DeNaples' trial surprisingly ended in a hung jury, and several years later, Bufalino underboss James Osticco was convicted of bribing a juror and fixing the trial.

DeNaples had other secrets, and to prepare for his background investigation, he hired a team of consultants, several of whom had close and long-standing ties to Governor Rendell. Among them were Kevin Feeley, who was Rendell's deputy mayor for communications during his tenure as Philadelphia's mayor, from 1992 to 2000. Feeley was a pro at crisis management, and given the potential pitfalls ahead for DeNaples, Feeley was the perfect choice to serve as a strategist and spokesman for DeNaples, especially when it would come time to publicly explain a recent episode in DeNaples' past known as the "exploding Katrina Trucks."

\* \* \*

THE FREIGHTLINER COLUMBIA tractor truck looked brand new. It had little mileage, was clean in and out and the engine purred. It also came with a clean title and full warranty and a price of $75,000, which was far below the $125,000 someone would usually pay for a similar truck. The reason for the discount, said the salesman, was that the truck had been in water, but not to worry because the water reached only halfway up the tires and never touched the engine.

Richard Rothstein thought he found a bargain he couldn't pass up, so in December 2005, he wrote a check to DeNaples Auto Sales, and for the next three months, he drove his new truck up and down I-81. Within weeks of his purchase, Rothstein developed a nasty cough that just wouldn't quit. So he hired a driver to work his route and then went to Florida to convalesce for a month or so.

But one cold night in March 2006 as the truck was heading north on I-81 with a new load, the engine burst into flames. The driver escaped injury, and the truck was taken to a local repair shop. Rothstein quickly returned home, but when he arrived at the auto shop, he was told that the "full warranty" he was given by DeNaples Auto Sales had been voided some six months earlier. The repair shop had some other news for Rothstein. When they removed the dashboard, mechanics found dead salamanders encased in dried mud, and there was mold throughout the cabin. The truck, said the mechanics, had been underwater.

Irate, Rothstein called DeNaples Auto Sales, which

agreed to buy the truck back for $68,000. But Rothstein was still perturbed, and he called the truck's manufacturer, Freightliner, to inquire about the truck and its history. Freightliner said the warranty had been voided in 2005 because the truck was one of thirty that had been parked in New Orleans and completely submerged by seawater when Hurricane Katrina struck. The trucks had been leased by Air Products and Chemicals of Trexlertown, Pennsylvania, and were at an Air Products facility when the hurricane hit and the levees subsequently broke, with the rushing water filling the Air Products lot with a toxic, oily paste.

Rothstein spoke to the chief mechanic at Air Products, who told him he had circled around the submerged trucks in a rowboat. The leasing company, LeasePlan USA, asked Air Products to help find someone who would buy the trucks at salvage, and one of those contacted was Louis DeNaples, who offered $180,000 for the thirty trucks, or $6,000 each. The check was originally written from DeNaples' Keystone Landfill Inc., but it was not accepted because LeasePlan required a check from a certified auto dealer. So the check was instead cut by DeNaples Auto Sales, with the paperwork clearly indicating that the trucks were water damaged and sold as salvage.

Designated a "flood vehicle," the truck was, by law, a salvage vehicle since it was submerged to the extent that vital parts such as the engine and transmission were exposed to water and damaged. Because a flood vehicle is not deemed operable, the insurance company settles the claim, and the trucks are sold at a discount.

Across the United States, flooded trucks and autos are part of a regular trade where, following natural disasters, they are brought to different states, cleaned up and sold to unsuspecting buyers. Because the engines and transmissions were under water, the vehicles often develop electrical problems and, as Rothstein's truck did, catch fire. The trick for a seller is getting a clear title from the state Department of Transportation. By not disclosing the damage, the sellers are committing a crime called "title washing," which is a felony. Somehow, DeNaples was able to register his trucks with the Pennsylvania Department of Transportation with clean titles, as if they were never destroyed by Hurricane Katrina. In Pennsylvania, a damaged or salvaged vehicle requires a *W* on its state title. But that wasn't the case with the Rothstein truck. Instead, the truck was put on the lot with a $75,000 price tag and advertised with a full warranty, which for the unsuspecting buyer had already been voided by Freightliner.

By the summer of 2006, Rothstein was still coughing and suffering from lung problems. Convinced he was sickened by the mold in the truck, he decided to share his story with investigators with the gaming board's Bureau of Investigations and Enforcement (BIE).

The FBI was also interested. Rothstein had originally contacted the Scranton office, but for some reason, the case was referred to the U.S. attorney in Binghamton, New York, about ninety miles north. After making several inquiries, prosecutors in Binghamton decided that titling was a state issue and referred the case back to Pennsylvania and to the state police.

When Ralph Periandi first heard the news about the Katrina flood trucks, he was floored. It had been eighteen months since his visit with the FBI in Philadelphia, and his "Black Ops" team had come up with information on DeNaples that was long on history but short on substance. The Katrina trucks solved that issue. Around the same time the Katrina truck incident fell into his lap, the police were pointed to two other DeNaples-related cases.

Agents from the gaming board's own BIE learned that DeNaples had been caught on an FBI wiretap talking to Shamsud-din Ali, a Philadelphia Imam who was under investigation for racketeering and defrauding the city of Philadelphia (he was later convicted and sent to prison).

Tensions between the state police and BIE continued to fester while Rendell sought to legitimize the gaming board's investigators within law enforcement circles. The legislature approved several laws that allowed BIE to share criminal background information, but none were recognized by either the police, attorney general, FBI or any other law enforcement agency. Periandi explained the police position in nearly a dozen letters to Tad Decker and to other gaming board members, but to no avail, as they demanded that the police cooperate. So the BIE referral was a sort of peace offering.

DeNaples was not the target of the Ali investigation, but he was notified by the FBI that he was inadvertently captured on the phone in a conversation recorded in July 2002. Others heard during the conversation were Jamie Brazil, a local Scranton political operative with deep ties that had stretched to the Clinton White House—he was a cousin of Hillary Clinton. The conversation with Ali centered on several matters, from DeNaples getting a plum parking spot for one of his daughters, who was about to attend college in Philadelphia, to transporting hazardous waste to his landfill.

Despite their cold relationship, BIE nevertheless alerted the state police to the wiretap, and the police in turn got a copy from the FBI. DeNaples could be heard clearly talking to Ali, Brazil and DeNaples' assistant Betty Kakareka.

*"Good morning. How you doing?" said Ali.*

*"Good morning. He is on the phone. I don't know if you can hold for a minute. I will try to get him off," said Kakareka.*

*"Yeah, we'll hold, cause it's good news," said Brazil.*

*"Okay, I did tell him you were going to call. I figured you'd be calling back. Hold on please."*

*"Hello?"*

*"Louis, this is Imam and Jamie Brazil on the line."*

*"Imam and Jamie, how are you?"*

*"Very good," said Ali. "It's good to talk to you again."*

*"It's good to talk to you. How's the family?"*

*"Everybody's good. How's everyone in your family?"*

*"Thank God, they're good."*

*"The Imam's got some good news for you, Louis," said Brazil.*

*"Anyway, we took care of that thing down at the university," said Ali.*

The "thing" was a parking space for DeNaples' daughter, who was planning to attend Temple University. The conversation moved to something more important to prosecutors. Once DeNaples was assured the parking spot was secured, the conversation moved to an urgent business matter involving the removal of hazardous debris from Philadelphia.

*"Louis I want to ask you a question,"* said Brazil. *"The Imam and I got a call about—and I don't know if it's a bogus call, or what's up with it—getting rid of all the debris from the homes they're tearing down in Philadelphia and nobody's accepting it. And I said you got to be kidding. Like no landfills—nobody's accepting this stuff?"*

*"We can definitely take it,"* said DeNaples. *"You know, me and you talked about this but it never materialized, remember?"*

*"Yeah, well, I got a call from, and between us, John Minora, saying he's got a buddy by the name of Ray someone, Rinaldi or something that can ship it by rail out to Ohio. And me and the Imam were talking, saying Jeez, I can't believe no one would take this stuff."*

*"No, we definitely could take it. In fact, we talked about you guys bringing it to us and nothing ever materialized—nobody ever contacted you?"*

*"Nobody, nothing ever happened."*

*"Shawn Fordham never called, called you?"*

*"We never—remember we had the meeting here. Nobody ever called me. In fact, we never got one ounce of*

material or business from that city of Philadelphia at all. We could definitely, definitely take that material."

"So Louis, you'd be willing to accept this?"

"Absolutely. Absolutely, in fact, it would be business for us and we'd be very appreciative if we got it."

"Yeah, because, you know, I mean I got Sam talking to the mayor to find out—"

"In fact, not only that, I got two landfills that I can take it in. I can take it into the CES, our other landfill in Schuylkill County."

"Now let's keep this between ourselves, cause when I got that call I thought to myself . . . I'll wait for you to call me. I'll do nothing till one of you people get back to me."

"Yeah, I'll find out if they are, they are having a hard problem getting rid of it. If they are, we know where it's going."

"Yeah, but even if they don't have a hard time getting rid of it maybe you can get something coming our way to help us a little and help everybody."

"That's right," said Ali.

"If we get helped, everybody gets helped, you know."

"The mayor thinks you are being taken care of, because after Sam and the Imam came up to visit you, they went right to the mayor's office, and right in front of them Shawn Fordham was supposed to call you."

"I can tell you right now that I had absolutely no conversation with anybody about any business at all other than when you people was in my office. And from that day on—"

"Nothing," said Ali.

> *"I had talked to absolutely nobody in Philadelphia
> about ten cents' worth of business," said DeNaples. "No-
> body called me and I didn't call them because—"*
>
> *"Hear that Iman?" said Brazil.*
>
> *"Yeah."*
>
> *"I'm the kind of guy that—I won't push," said De-
> Naples. "I'm not a pushy guy—you know that there."*

The tape was an important piece of evidence, given
DeNaples' denials the previous summer that he had
known Ali. He had been questioned twice, in August and
September 2006, by BIE attorneys about his relationship
with Ali, and the investigators knew they had trapped him
in a lie. The tape and the Katrina truck probe were damning enough, but then came word that the feds had reeled
in a very big fish.

ON OCTOBER 12, 2006, the U.S. Department of Homeland Security and the state police executed a warrant to
search the home and car of William "Big Billy" D'Elia.

D'Elia had been previously charged in May with laundering drug money and was free awaiting trial, but he
apparently used his freedom to hire a hit man to kill the
confidential informant who provided the information that
led to the charges against him. The ongoing investigation
was of such importance that the government approved
cash transfers of up to $50,000 to snare Big Billy.

Following Russell Bufalino's death, in 1994, D'Elia
remained one of the primary organized crime targets in

the state, along with Joey Merlino, of Philadelphia's Bruno family, and Sonny Ciancutti, who led the Pittsburgh mob.

For nearly a decade, the state police had been investigating D'Elia in an attempt to tie up many of the loose ends still hanging from several previous and unsuccessful probes into his activities. Although those cases went nowhere, investigators did cultivate new confidential informants, which resulted in better leads and information, which clearly pointed to direct links between D'Elia and DeNaples.

The police knew, for instance, through routine surveillance that D'Elia regularly visited DeNaples at his auto parts business in Dunmore. D'Elia typically drove around to the back and walked in through a private entrance. The police also had surveillance photos of DeNaples taken at D'Elia's daughter's wedding, and they also had video of the pair at the auto parts store.

At six feet four inches and well over 250 pounds, D'Elia was an intimidating figure, though his special talent wasn't with a gun but his ability to talk and negotiate. D'Elia had been a soldier with the Bufalino family since the 1960s and was one of the last of the Bufalino family members to be "made," or officially inducted into the organized crime family. During his years at Bufalino's side, D'Elia made the kind of contacts an up-and-coming wise guy could only dream of. There were lunches and dinners in Philadelphia and introductions to the leaders of New York's five families and their counterparts across the river in New Jersey. Over time, D'Elia emerged as a trusted figure who could facilitate peace for gangsters throughout the northeast and other parts of the country. D'Elia's negotiating ability led to his appointment by Bufalino as the point man for conducting family business during Bufalino's imprisonment through the 1980s.

It wasn't so much that the other mob families respected D'Elia but that he was representing Russell Bufalino, and D'Elia was called to Pittsburgh, Philadelphia, New Jersey and New York to voice his opinion in family and business conflicts, opinions everyone knew in reality were the wishes of Bufalino.

After Bufalino died, it was D'Elia who was in charge of all family business, most important, its vast gambling operation.

Gambling was for decades a mainstay for Bufalino family income, with associates taking wagers throughout the region on all professional and college sports. Like other mob families, the Bufalinos charged a "vigorish," or interest payment for taking a bet, much like a credit-card company charges a fee for taking a cash advance at an ATM machine.

In most cases, the "vig" was 5 to 10 percent of the bet. So if someone bet $100, he'd pay a $5 to $10 fee no matter the outcome, win or lose. The idea was to take an equal amount of bets on a game. If the betting was one-sided, a portion would be "laid off" to mob families in other cities willing to take the action.

Bufalino family gambling operations centered in Pennsylvania and central New York State, but there were also associates handling accounts in New Jersey, New York City and Massachusetts, and the monthly proceeds often reached into the mid–six figures, and sometimes more. Law enforcement had from time to time tried to get a handle on the Bufalino family gambling operation. Every now and then, there would be a minor arrest, but it wasn't until long after Russell Bufalino's death, in 1994, that a joint federal–state police probe revealed the true depth of the operation. That investigation, explored in a 2001 federal affidavit, revealed the results of a long-standing probe into D'Elia and several associates.

From the mid-1980s through 2000, Bufalino family couriers were transporting the cash in an elaborate and organized fashion in which rental cars were used to drive to preselected pickup locations from Massachusetts to western Pennsylvania and all points in between.

Cash-filled bags would be placed in the cars, and the money would be taken to drop-off points, usually truck stops off of major highways. Among the most popular drop-off points was the Columbia truck stop off of I-80 on the New Jersey side of the Delaware Water Gap, which was about an hour's drive west of New York City. Couriers, who were paid as much as $10,000 per week, were told to get "gas" if there was a pickup scheduled at the truck stop or "something to eat" if the pickup was inside the restaurant.

Often the bags would contain as much as $200,000 in $50 and $100 bills. The volume was extraordinary, and by the late 1990s, much of the gambling proceeds were being laundered through the casinos in Atlantic City.

According to one informant, the laundering operation consisted of D'Elia giving him upward of $200,000 in small-denomination bills, usually fives, tens and twenties. The money would be counted and placed into $500 bundles, after which a half a dozen or so women would drive to Atlantic City with money in hand and visit each of the casinos there. They would all buy $5,000 worth of chips, wait a little while, and then cash them in. One rule was to never cash more than $10,000, which would necessitate reporting the money to the Internal Revenue Service.

It usually took about half a day to hit all of the casinos, but when they were done, the group members successfully laundered their gambling proceeds. When they returned to Pennsylvania, they handed the "clean" money to D'Elia, usually at the Mountain Top home of a friend.

The Atlantic City laundering operation came to a sudden end in 2003, when the New Jersey state gaming commission got wise to the scheme and identified D'Elia as a member of organized crime. He was slapped with a lifetime ban from entering any of the state's casinos.

Gambling wasn't D'Elia's only source of income. Though he was not convicted of any crimes, the FBI developed intelligence revealing that D'Elia may have had other lucrative businesses that included the acquisition and sale of stolen merchandise, particularly gold, diamonds and clothing. At times he also had his gambling couriers transport drugs, usually cocaine. D'Elia had also for years been involved in the solid-waste business as a "waste broker" who sold air rights at landfills, including the Keystone Landfill owned by Louis DeNaples.

It was D'Elia who steered trash haulers in New York City and Philadelphia owned by other mob families to Keystone Landfill. The police had always heard stories from their informants about bodies being dumped at the landfill, victims who crossed Mafiosi throughout the region. No remains were ever found, and no one was ever charged.

D'Elia held a firearms permit and was usually carrying a gun. He owned sixteen guns, including a 12-gauge shotgun, two .44 caliber handguns and a 9 mm Uzi submachine gun.

The investigation that finally led to D'Elia's arrest was headed by U.S. Homeland Security special agent Maureen Meschke and state police trooper Dave Swartz, a thirteen-year veteran who was a criminal investigator with BCI and a key member of its Organized Crime Task Force before joining the gaming investigation with Weinstock.

They first learned in October 2005 that D'Elia was involved in a new laundering scheme. D'Elia was lured to a meeting in Hazleton with a police informant who sought D'Elia's help in wiring $100,000 in what he claimed was drug money to the Dominican Republic to pay for the smuggling of two illegal aliens to the states.

D'Elia agreed, and his conversation was recorded by the informant.

"Do you want me to give you cash or certified check?"

"Cash is good," said D'Elia, "anything, cash, wire transfer, I can tell you what to do and where to send it."

"No, I cannot show the money, it's illegal money, it's drug money."

"You don't have to tell me, buddy," said D'Elia. "You don't have to tell me any secrets. Give me cash and we'll do it when you're ready."

The two men spoke again on May 12, and that conversation was also recorded. The two men agreed to make the money transfer at the Woodlands, a restaurant and catering hall in Wilkes-Barre. Prior to the meeting, the police gave the informant $50,000 in a Cingular Wireless bag, which he put in the trunk of his car. When he arrived at the Woodlands parking lot, the informant took the bag out and gave it to D'Elia, who had parked nearby. He in turn put the bag in the trunk of his black Lincoln Town Car and drove away.

They met again on May 16 at a pizza restaurant in Mountain Top to talk about the wire transfer and to pay D'Elia $2,500, which was his 5 percent cut, or "points," for facilitating the transfer. Ten days later, on May 26, D'Elia called the informant to say that the transfer had been completed, and D'Elia gave the informant the account information. Unbeknownst to D'Elia, a grand jury had subpoenaed the bank records, which showed that the money was sent from a Citizens Bank account that belonged to longtime D'Elia associate Robert Kulick and his wife, Michelle Mattioli-Kulick, who happened to be the daughter of Joseph Mattioli, the longtime owner of Pocono Raceway.

On June 16, D'Elia met again with the informant at the pizza restaurant to collect the other $50,000, which was stuffed inside a Walmart bag. They left the restaurant in separate cars, and the informant, under police surveillance, followed D'Elia to an abandoned building in an industrial park, where the informant handed over the Walmart bag.

By October, D'Elia learned that the wire transfers were part of a federal probe and that investigators had questioned several people, including Kulick. D'Elia met again with the informant, who feigned anger and sought D'Elia's help in killing the contact in the Dominican Republic who supposedly received the wire transfers along with another $300,000 the informant claimed to have given him.

"He fucked us for $400,000 and we're going to find him," said the informant.

D'Elia offered to help find the man, and, with their conversation again recorded, D'Elia learned at a subsequent meeting that the Dominican contact was partners with a Russian who was part of a human-trafficking ring that imported Russian women to appear in pornography films.

"So when my guys get him, what do you want them to do with him?"

"If I decide to kill this guy, do you have the people over there to wipe him out overnight?" said the informant.

"Yeah," said D'Elia. "You just gotta tell me what to do."

D'Elia didn't agree to kill the man. Instead, he offered to find and detain him so "you go do what you want with him. You get the money out of him, whatever you want."

But the informant persisted and offered D'Elia $200,000 to "take this guy down."

"I gotcha," said D'Elia.

The informant later gave D'Elia a photograph of the

bogus Dominican smuggler and $5,000 to pay for the travel expenses of D'Elia's men. That led investigators to obtain a search warrant of D'Elia's home as their investigation morphed from money laundering to murder-for-hire.

The search of D'Elia's home produced a treasure trove of information, including nearly three-dozen assorted guns, bullets and magazines, cell phones, bank records from First National Community Bank and a phone book with the numbers of various associates, among them the home number of Louis DeNaples.

In November 2006, D'Elia was charged in a superseding indictment with conspiring to kill a witness. His bail was revoked and he was sent to a prison in Pike County, which straddled the New Jersey border in northeastern Pennsylvania. D'Elia, now sixty, was facing charges that would keep him in prison for life, and he didn't waste any time agreeing to cooperate with the government and firing his longtime counsel, Philip Gelso, whose father Charles had for years represented Russell Bufalino.

The deal was such that D'Elia agreed to cooperate with any federal, state or local investigation. To replace Gelso, the court appointed James Swetz, a notable Stroudsburg defense attorney who gained fame in the 1990s for the acquittal of a Stroudsburg police chief accused of looting the town's parking meters. With D'Elia now cooperating, the first order of business was to have him tell the state police everything he knew about Louis DeNaples.

*   *   *

THE FBI WIRETAP and Katrina trucks were open criminal investigations, yet somehow, in the middle of December 2006, the state Gaming Control Board unanimously determined that Louis DeNaples was "suitable" to receive a slots license. The board knew about Katrina and the wiretap from their own BIE investigators yet looked the other way.

The police had also gotten wind that suspected DeNaples had given Ed Rendell large contributions over the past few months, more than $100,000, which the board also ignored.

A week before the board would officially announce the new casino licensees, two of its investigators, Roger Greenback and Jack Meighan, asked the U.S. attorney's office for permission to interview Billy D'Elia. Greenback, BIE's eastern regional director, and Meighan, an agent in the office, had worked for months on DeNaples' background investigative report and thought they had more than enough to convince the board it couldn't award DeNaples a slots license.

Greenback was a former FBI agent who once investigated organized crime in Pittsburgh, and Meighan was also a retired FBI agent who had worked in Pittsburgh. Tasked with completing DeNaples' background check, the two investigators spent weeks on the ground interviewing dozens of people, and in their final report, they included a host of damning information—from the 2001 federal affidavit linking DeNaples' and D'Elia's business interests, to D'Elia's regular visits to DeNaples' office at his auto parts facility, to DeNaples' attendance at the wedding of D'Elia's daughter.

But the information did little to convince the board that DeNaples wasn't "suitable," so with time running out, Greenback and Meighan contacted the U.S. attorney's office in Harrisburg and requested to interview D'Elia. But the request was denied. The FBI, in a letter previously sent to the gaming board in February 2006, had reasserted its position that it wouldn't cooperate with BIE, which was still deemed by law enforcement as a civilian agency and thus not privy to criminal information. The U.S. attorney's office in turn would not allow investigators with a licensing agency to interview D'Elia.

Shut out from D'Elia, the two former FBI agents could only watch with dismay on December 22, 2006, as the gaming board unanimously awarded Louis DeNaples a slots license.

The decision had come with some drama, as word leaked that one member of the gaming board, Ken McCabe, would vote against the DeNaples application. McCabe was a former FBI agent who had worked in Pittsburgh and was said to have genuine concerns about DeNaples. When the seven-member board voted, McCabe paused before giving his vote to approve DeNaples.

At state police headquarters, Ralph Periandi wasn't surprised. The DeNaples gaming license was a foregone conclusion, just as he had predicted during his initial meeting with the FBI in April 2005. But the state police now had enough information on DeNaples that during the weeks following the slots decision, Periandi put the machinery in place that would result in a grand jury investigation. The venue would be in Harrisburg. Periandi had his misgivings about the state attorney general's office and decided early on that any prosecutions that evolved from a state police investigation into gaming would be handled in Dauphin County and by its district attorney Ed Marsico.

Periandi remained deeply disturbed over how the state's political apparatus mobilized in such a way that even someone with DeNaples' checkered history could be cleansed and given the stamp of approval. Periandi also remained concerned over other issues relating to gaming, including the hiring of several vendors that were close to the Rendell administration, among them G-Tech, a firm that Periandi had discussed during his initial meeting with the FBI.

G-Tech was a global company that operated lotteries in nearly two-dozen states and a number of foreign countries and had been accused elsewhere of bribing officials to gain lucrative contracts.

Nearly a decade earlier, in 1996, G-Tech's then national sales director, J. David Smith, was convicted of fraud for taking nearly $170,000 from lobbyists in New Jersey. G-Tech also had problems in Texas, where criminal investigators with the Texas Department of Public Safety alleged in a 2006 report that G-Tech bribed lottery officials there and in several foreign countries, including Poland, Brazil, Trinidad and Tobago and the Czech Republic. No criminal charges were filed, but the report said G-Tech was an "aggressive business entity that had a past history . . . of pursuing new contracts with sometimes questionable actions."

It wasn't lost on Periandi that Ken Jarin, one of Rendell's closest confidants, was hired by G-Tech in 2003 to serve as a consultant and successfully brought in the lucrative state gaming contract. Just six days after G-Tech was awarded that contract, the firm made a $50,000 donation to the Democratic Governors Association, for which Jarin served as treasurer. The same group had given Rendell $462,000 for his gubernatorial run in 2002.

Department of Revenue secretary Greg Fajt deflected any criticism of G-Tech's contract away from Rendell, saying it was his decision and his alone to award the firm the contract. In his press release announcing G-Tech's hiring, Fajt said the contract was worth less than $7 million. In truth, over the course of the five years, the contract would eventually pay out closer to $40 million, and much more once the contract was renewed.

Even more ominous, under gaming board chairman Tad Decker's direction, G-Tech was also tasked with working with BIE on background investigations of potential casino employees. To Periandi, all that meant was the administration through G-Tech would get a heads-up on the status of all background investigations. Periandi had wanted to know more about the firm, but Decker prevented the state police from performing a mandatory background check despite a requirement that every vendor had to be vetted, with every principal submitting to a background review. But that wasn't to be the case with G-Tech.

# SEVEN

James Riddle Hoffa was a fast-rising union organizer for the International Brotherhood of Teamsters union. Born in Indiana in 1913, Hoffa's father was a coal miner who died in 1920 of black-lung disease. His mother moved the family in 1922 to Detroit where, at fourteen, Hoffa dropped out of school and worked as a manual laborer, but he later showed promise as a union organizer while working at Kroger Grocery and Baking Company unloading fruit and vegetables from trains. Hoffa earned thirty-two cents an hour, much of it in company credit to exchange for groceries. The shifts were twelve hours long and began in the late afternoon, but workers were only paid for the time they actually unloaded goods.

In 1931, in the midst of the Great Depression, with bread lines found on virtually every corner, Hoffa led his first work stoppage after two friends were fired for walking off the premises to eat their dinner. Truckloads of Florida strawberries had just arrived and needed to be placed in refrigerators, but Hoffa resisted and supplied a list of demands, which included a thirteen-cents–per-hour raise, guaranteed pay for half a day, medical insurance and Kroger's recognition of the workers union, which would soon apply for and receive a charter as Federal Local 19341 of the American Federation of Labor.

Hoffa lost his job a year later after he punched a plant foreman, but his burgeoning reputation earned him a position with the International Brotherhood of Teamsters Local 299. Hoffa didn't receive a salary. Instead, he earned a percentage of the dues each new member would pay to join the union, which amounted to a $10 initiation fee and $2 per month. Hoffa jumped into his new job with gusto, organizing workers throughout Detroit, visiting warehouses, loading docks and stopping at truck stops to preach the union way. The work was dangerous and often violent, as union organizers often found themselves in confrontations with the police and thugs hired by the very businesses Hoffa sought to unionize. During his first year, by his own account, Hoffa was clubbed, punched or hit with brass knuckles three dozen times.

The number of beatings nearly matched his arrest record. Hoffa would show up on picket lines, where he'd be arrested, brought to the police station, released and then return back to the picket line. During one twenty-four-hour period, Hoffa was arrested eighteen times.

When Hoffa wasn't picketing, he was driving up and down country highways, approaching long-haul drivers while they slept. He perfected his rat-a-tat introduction of "Hi, I'm Jimmy Hoffa of the Teamsters" and would say it quickly before stepping back to show the driver he wasn't there to rob him. Of course, sometimes the truckers were really toughs hired by the trucking companies to rough up Hoffa.

Along with the head, facial and body wounds suffered from his duties, Hoffa was the target of several car bombings, and he developed the habit to never close the door when starting his car. He'd leave his left leg hanging out, believing he'd simply get blown out of the car and thus improve his chances for survival if the car exploded. Hoffa's fearlessness, boundless enthusiasm and belief in the union way endeared him to the men he was recruiting. He also benefited financially from signing the new members.

A decade later, Hoffa was running Detroit Teamsters Local 299, and his rise to power coincided with a partnership that not only provided the muscle to help inflict his will, but one that would follow him through the rest of his days.

And it was through that alliance that Hoffa first met William Bufalino.

William Bufalino first appeared in Detroit during the summer of 1946. The son of a coal miner, Bufalino was born in 1918 and was one of nine children raised in Pittston, Pennsylvania. He studied for two years to become a Catholic priest before deciding on a career as an attorney. After serving in the U.S. Army's Judge Advocate Corps during World War II, William arrived in Michigan under orders from his older cousin.

Since 1940, Detroit had served as one of the strategic import centers for narcotics arriving from Italy. Detroit's harbor and central location provided easy distribution throughout the Midwest, and the members of the "Detroit Partnership," the organized crime group coheaded by Angelo Meli, used their money from the lucrative drug trade to fuel other businesses, including jukeboxes and labor racketeering.

Meli's narcotic connections linked him closely to New York mobsters, who shared in the lucrative drug trade, and in 1941, the alliance found another source of revenue, thanks to Jimmy Hoffa and the International Brotherhood of Teamsters. During Hoffa's rise from union organizer to president of Detroit Teamsters Local 299, he was locked in a death struggle with the Congress of Industrial Organizations (CIO). He needed help, and he turned to Santo Perrone, the Detroit crime boss, and Meli.

Raised in Detroit, Meli was a gangster almost by birth, and by the 1930s, he had consolidated his power, eventually serving as consigliere to the Detroit family. He was also among the first organized crime figures to be aligned with Jimmy Hoffa's Teamsters Local 299.

When William Bufalino arrived in Detroit, he came with $30,000, with half coming from a Pittston bank and the remainder from his cousin, Russell. The money was used to invest in the Bilvin Distributing Company, which placed jukeboxes throughout the region but also served as a front for Russell, Meli and a host of other underworld associates. Within two years after arriving in Detroit, William had settled in, even marrying Angelo Meli's niece,

Marie Antoinette Meli, and the marriage united the Bufalino and Meli families. It was typically Sicilian yet
proved to be a pivotal event, given that the Bufalinos were
now firmly cemented in Detroit and focused on a bigger
prize—the Teamsters union.

In 1948, William gave up his interests in the jukebox
company and was named president of Detroit Teamsters
Local 985, which in reality was headed by Hoffa. Sharp-
tongued, the younger Bufalino was the perfect choice to
lead the Bufalino family's interests in Detroit, and he
would keep his cousin Russell abreast of everything there
was to know regarding the Teamsters, and Jimmy Hoffa.

BY THE TIME the Kefauver Committee issued its final
report, in 1951, Russell Bufalino was fully in charge of
the Pittston family.

His rise had been facilitated by a variety of factors. He
was smart, organized and maintained the lowest of pro-
files. He also had the counsel of Santo Volpe and his uncle
Charles Bufalino, the two aging leaders who transformed
the Wyoming Valley years earlier through bribes and murder. Most important, Bufalino had the support of his old
mentor, don Stefano Magaddino of Buffalo.

Following Prohibition, Magaddino remained a force
within organized crime circles. He still had a seat on the
Commission, and his business interests remained far and
wide and included tribute that came from the Scranton
region through Bufalino.

As a student of Magaddino, Bufalino never showed any

visible signs of wealth. He lived in a modest ranch-style home he purchased for $22,000. He dressed plainly, drove an older car and, because of a cataract problem, he often had someone drive him from one appointment to another. His local business interests, aside from the garment factories, included restaurants, hotels, banks and jewelry shops. The student was also trained to be ruthless, and he dispatched enemies quickly and quietly, relying on a core group of killers.

Yet outside his "family" pursuits, Bufalino treated civilians with kindness and respect. On one occasion, Bufalino spotted an elderly neighbor working on his roof in the middle of a sweltering summer day. Within minutes several brawny men arrived and told the man to get down.

"Mr. Bufalino says you shouldn't be working up there on such a hot day and we should finish the job for you," said one of the men.

Known as "McGee" by those closest to him, Bufalino cultivated politicians and took care of local police departments, either through cash handouts or favors. Upon arriving home from New York every Wednesday, Bufalino made a point of having dinner with his wife, Carrie, and close friends, but he only visited restaurants that he owned or was sure of the quality of its fare. Bufalino loved food and the artistry of creating a good meal. There was the red wine, which he used to dip his prosciutto bread, a main course of chicken or fish and always the pasta with the "gravy," or sauce. When he wasn't eating in a familiar restaurant, Bufalino would entertain by cooking special meals. Food was just more than eating. It was an opportunity to communicate, to talk, to enjoy the company of friends or to discuss issues with associates and underlings relating to his myriad of business interests.

In addition to his hold over the Scranton area and interests in New York, Bufalino also spent time in Philadelphia with his good friend Angelo Bruno, whose father ran the Philly mob until his death, in 1946.

Bruno remained an important member of the family and was in line to become its boss, but he was content developing and nurturing his many business interests and those he shared with Bufalino. The two men had similar personality traits. Both were quiet and operated behind the scenes, though Bruno was more of a conciliator than Bufalino. Later known as "the Gentle Don," Bruno preferred to negotiate a problem but wouldn't hesitate to use violence as the means to an end.

Along with his hold over the garment industry, Bufalino's rising influence within the Teamsters union provided him with a powerful platform. He and Bruno shared a hold over the Teamsters, though Bruno's interest was the Philadelphia local, while Bufalino had inroads in the national organization through his cousin William and Jimmy Hoffa.

By the mid-1950s, Bufalino was earning 5 percent for every Teamsters loan he'd facilitate for friends and business associates from the Central States pension fund, and as Hoffa rose through the national union, so too did Bufalino's fortunes. His placement of cousin William in Detroit in 1946 was a genius stroke, and William's subsequent appointment to lead Jimmy Hoffa's Detroit Teamsters

Local 985 brought Russell Bufalino closer to the bombastic, up-and-coming Hoffa as their relationship grew deeper, and profitable.

Bufalino liked Hoffa. He was tough, had a good business mind and, above all, was a man of his word. But because of the attention brought by the Kefauver Committee, a new U.S. House subcommittee in 1953, chaired by Representative Clare E. Hoffman, began investigating racketeering in Detroit. The Hoffman Committee focused on Hoffa and his local 985 president, William Bufalino. In its report, the committee discovered the true dealings behind the Detroit local.

> *There existed a gigantic, wicked conspiracy to, through the use of force, threats of force and economic pressure, extort and collect millions of dollars not only from unorganized workers but from members of unions who are in good standing, from independent businessmen, and, on occasion, from the Federal Government itself. . . . The Teamsters union, Local 985, through its president William E. Bufalino, is the principal offender and perpetrator of the racketeering, extortion, and gangsterism.*

Despite its report, the committee did little to upset organized crime's control over the union or its influence with Hoffa and the Teamsters. Still, the FBI had no choice but to quietly acknowledge that the mob did exist, and J. Edgar Hoover ordered the bureau to begin the Top Hoodlum Program.

Agents in cities across America were told to document

the activities of the nation's top organized crime figures, and that included Bufalino, with his first reports filed by agents trailing him in Pittston, New York and Philadelphia. A year later, the bureau had accumulated enough information to produce an initial report for its Philadelphia Top Hoodlum file.

> *[Russell Bufalino] is the nephew of Charles Bufalino, alleged to be one of the two most powerful men in the Mafia of the Pittston, Pa. area. . . . Russell Bufalino is the active leader of the Mafia, with his uncle Charles and Santo Volpe acting as silent partners. . . . We are advised that during World War II, Bufalino was employed as a mechanic in a bottling plant operated by Joseph Barbara in Binghamton, N.Y. Bufalino is married and resides at 720 Wyoming Street, Exeter, which is near Pittston, Pa. . . . Bufalino, as the alleged head of the Mafia in the Pittston area, has gained control of approximately seven dress factories in that area and apparently has a "hold" on all persons involved in gambling activities in the Pittston area, in that he, Bufalino, gets a "cut" from each of them.*
>
> *During April of 1953 . . . there were approximately 40 dress factories in and around Pittston, Pa. About half of these factories are operated by individuals from the New York City area, about whom background information was not available to the informant. The remaining half are operated by individuals from the Pittston area and have been infiltrated and dominated by known racketeers and hoodlums headed by [Bufalino]. Infor-*

*mant stated that it was his understanding that anyone*
*who desired to enter this field had to make arrangements*
*through Bufalino, who has contacts in New York City, to*
*obtain contracts for dresses. In return, Bufalino received*
*a certain percentage of each dress manufactured under*
*the contract.*

Aside from his contacts with Santo Volpe and Charles Bufalino, the report linked Bufalino to several other mobsters, including Bruno. Agents tracked Bufalino to hangouts such as the Imperial Poolroom in Pittston and an office he used near the Martz bus terminal in Scranton. They also followed him on his weekly trips to New York City, where he routinely stayed at the Hotel Forrester, with side trips to the Hotel Lexington and the Hotel New Yorker.

Bufalino usually flew to New York from the airport in Avoca, Pennsylvania, near Scranton on Monday morning and returned to Pennsylvania on Wednesday. The report said that Bufalino ran all gambling activity in the region, including betting on football, baseball, basketball and crap games.

Bufalino's closest friend, according to the FBI, was William Medico, the owner of the Medico Electric Company. Medico allegedly made his money in bootlegging during Prohibition and subsequently moved to legitimate and illegitimate businesses. Medico was described as a capo in the Bufalino family, and there was wide suspicion that it was Bufalino who actually owned the Medico firm.

By 1956, the FBI was trailing Bufalino regularly and

even followed him, Medico and James Osticco, Bufalino's underboss, to Cuba, where they were spotted meeting with Santo Trafficante Jr. the South Florida Mafia boss who co-owned the Sans Souci night club. Bufalino remained there for a month. Medico later denied having been on the trip, but he forgot that he returned via the Bahamas, from where the FBI recovered a postcard he sent on May 5, 1956, which was stamped with the mark of the British Empire, which controlled the islands.

The 1956 trip wasn't the first time Bufalino had been to Cuba, but it was the first in which Bufalino had been followed to Cuba. Havana was a bustling city, alive with its casinos and nightlife, and unbeknownst to the FBI, Russell Bufalino wasn't just some tourist.

# EIGHT

In December 1946, the heads of all the organized crime families in the United States were summoned by Lucky Luciano to meet at the Hotel Nacional, in Havana.

Luciano had been imprisoned at the beginning of World War II following a conviction on a pandering charge, but he later struck an agreement to help the U.S. government by having his men keep an eye on the East Coast docks and waterfronts for German saboteurs. When the war ended, Luciano was rewarded with a pardon by New York governor Thomas E. Dewey but ordered to leave the country.

Luciano departed for Italy, where years earlier he saw the potential for heroin, particularly the vast, virgin market in the United States. Following the war, Luciano summoned the families to Havana to discuss, strategize and organize the flow of narcotics from Italy into the United

States. Luciano also had another subject on the agenda, and that was to resolve some festering issues that resulted from the return of Vito Genovese.

The meeting was considered historic, given the sheer numbers and power of those in attendance, which included Frank Costello, Albert Anastasia and Stefano Magaddino, who brought with him several underlings from the Buffalo and Scranton families, including Russell Bufalino.

Then in his early forties, Bufalino was a recognized leader, operating as an underboss to his brother-in-law John Sciandra but expanding his own power and influence beyond Pennsylvania and into New York City. Bufalino remained behind the scenes in Havana while the family leaders ironed out agreements on the drug trade, with the Italian heroin shipped to Havana and then brought into the United States.

Cuba was rapidly becoming a central business center for organized crime. The small country had a large identity problem due chiefly to the ever-changing political landscape, thanks in part to a former Cuban army sergeant who led a revolt in 1933.

After ascending to power, Ruben Fulgencio Batista Zaldívar subsequently gained the favor of the U.S. government, which recognized his new government in 1934. Handpicked presidents headed a puppet regime for several years before Batísta won the first election in 1940 under Cuba's newly devised constitution. Batista lost the presidency in 1944, but by then he had developed a business partnership with organized crime, which subsequently used that foothold to buy and build new hotels and casinos to lure tourists from the United States and Europe.

After losing the election, Batista divided his time over the next four years traveling from Cuba to Florida and New York, where he maintained residences and nurtured friendships. And among those he developed deep friendships with in the United States was Russell Bufalino. When Batista retook control of the country in a coup in 1952, his government was immediately recognized by President Dwight Eisenhower, and within months, he reached agreements with the Mafiosi and several American corporations, promising to match dollar for dollar any investment over $1 million in a hotel and casino. The point man for the organized crime interests was Meyer Lansky, a Jewish gangster allied with Luciano who was now the brains behind the entire Cuban operation.

As Cuba's economy, and fortunes, improved, so too did the fortunes of its corrupt president. Batista secured a cut, typically 10 percent to 30 percent, of casino revenues. He also took bribes from U.S. companies eager to win contracts for various construction projects, including those for new airports and highways. The astonishing cash infusion led Cuba to quickly become a playground for the wealthy, and at its height, the money flowing through the island produced a take for the mob that exceeded $1 million per day from the casinos alone. Lansky, ever the businessman, insisted that the spoils from Cuba be shared, and nearly every major organized crime boss in the United

States would have some interest in a Cuban hotel and casino, including the Sans Souci, Sevilla-Biltmore, Commodoro, Deauville, Capri, Nacional and Plaza.

Russell Bufalino was no exception, and he counted pieces of the Sans Souci and the Plaza hotels along with co-ownership of a dog track and a shrimping business. But Bufalino also had something the other mob leaders didn't have—a long-standing friendship with Batista. The two men had become so close that during the hot Cuban summers, Batista would send his children to northeastern Pennsylvania to vacation under Bufalino's protection.

By 1956, Bufalino's lucrative business interests included his holdings in Cuba; his infiltration of the Teamsters union, particularly its Central States pension fund; his choke hold over the garment industry; and a host of other businesses in Pennsylvania and New York. He was also the recognized leader of the northeastern Pennsylvania family, having taken over for John Sciandra in 1949. Joseph Barbara still ran New York's southern tier, but he was in ill health, having suffered two heart attacks within a year.

Now in his midfifties, Bufalino was duly recognized by other mob leaders as one of the most important gangsters in the country. Yet few outside organized crime circles knew or heard of him, and those who did had a hard time understanding why a crime boss from Kingston, Pennsylvania, could wield more power than a boss from New York or Chicago. But he did, which is why Bufalino was called upon to quell what could have been the greatest mob war since 1931.

\* \* \*

IT WAS MIDAFTERNOON on November 13, 1957, when New York State Police sergeant Edgar Croswell and trooper Vincent Vasisko arrived at the Parkway Motel on Route 17 near Binghamton, New York. They had been called to investigate a bad-check charge, and once inside the motel, Croswell recognized a man talking to the motel owners, Warren and Helen Schroeder. It was Joseph Barbara's son, Joseph Barbara Jr.

Croswell was all too familiar with the elder Barbara and his business interests in central New York. Barbara Sr. had lived in the region for nearly two decades. He owned a Canada Dry bottling plant and several other legitimate businesses. But Croswell knew about Barbara's history as a contract killer in Buffalo for Stefano Magaddino before relocating to central New York in the mid-1930s.

And if anyone doubted his violent side, they just had to look at his arrest record. Barbara had been picked up by the Pennsylvania State Police and charged with murdering a Sicilian from Montedoro, Calogero Calamera, on January 4, 1931. Calamera was walking along a Pittston street for a late-night walk when he was approached by two men and shot six times. Before he died, he told police he had outstanding issues with Santo Volpe and Charles Bufalino and gave descriptions of the two men who shot him. Police arrested Barbara, but later dropped the charges.

Barbara was arrested again a year later, again on suspicion of murder, but that charge was later withdrawn when a witness recanted. In February 1933, Barbara was arrested yet again after the body of a bootlegger and hijacker, Samuel Wichner, was found in the trunk of a car in Scranton with a noose around his neck and the other end of the rope fastened to his knees. Before his demise, Wichner had told his wife he met with Barbara at his home the night before to discuss a bootlegging business venture with Barbara and Santo Volpe but was told to come back the following night.

Barbara was charged again with murder, but like his other arrests, the charge was later dropped due to lack of evidence.

In 1946, six years after assuming control of the central New York territory, Barbara was charged with illegal acquisition of sugar, which was used to make alcohol. He was found guilty and fined $5,000. Following that arrest, he remained out of sight and spent much of his time at his estate in nearby Apalachin, a small hamlet just west of Binghamton that played host to several important meetings. In 1956, men in silk suits and late-model cars converged on the Barbara estate. The official reason was to pay their respects to Barbara after he suffered a heart attack, but Croswell learned Barbara hosted a meeting of the Commission, the appointed national leadership of *La Cosa Nostra*, which brought the heads of the five most important families throughout the United States and representatives from other families to his home to discuss business. The estate was in the country, with little if any police presence and isolated from the big cities. It was also a relatively easy commute from Buffalo for Stefano

Magaddino, who remained a powerful force within organized crime and served as the de facto host.

Barbara had also used his home for important meetings within his own family and lent it out to others to iron out intrafamily disputes. For nearly two years, men flew into the Binghamton airport and registered in local hotels under assumed names to meet at the Barbara estate.

When Barbara's son left the Parkway Motel on November 13, 1957, Croswell asked Mrs. Schroeder about her conversation. She said that Barbara Jr. had reserved three rooms for that night and the next and that the rooms were held under his father's Canada Dry Bottling Company. Barbara didn't say who the rooms were for but said the men were part of a Canada Dry convention his father was hosting at his home.

Suspicious, Croswell and Vasisko waited till dusk before driving to Barbara Sr.'s Apalachin home. They followed the single road as it wound up toward a hilltop, and when the troopers arrived, they spotted several cars, all with out-of-state license plates. The troopers quickly copied the plate numbers and, upon returning to their barracks, sent the numbers by teletype to the Binghamton office of the U.S. Treasury's Alcohol and Tobacco Tax Unit. While waiting for a reply, they went back to the Parkway Motel, where they spotted a Cadillac. After writing down that plate number, they went inside to talk to Mr. Schroeder and asked if he could get one of Barbara's guests to sign a registration card. Schroeder said that Barbara left implicit instructions that none of his guests were to sign and that he'd take care of the bill the following morning.

The troopers returned to their car and waited outside the motel until 2:30 A.M. They came back around noon the next day with an agent from the Alcohol and Tobacco Tax unit. They had learned that the Cadillac, which was still parked, belonged to the Buckeye Cigarette Service Company Inc., of Cleveland, Ohio. Croswell went inside the motel but was told by Mr. Schroeder that all of Barbara's guests had departed. The troopers rushed to the Canada Dry bottling plant, and then to Barbara's home in Apalachin.

The single-lane road split into two driveways near the house, with one leading to a four-car garage and side parking lot, while the other driveway wrapped around the home to a backyard barn. The estate itself was ranch style and made of stone. Several cars were parked in the front, and the troopers were jotting down some of the numbers from the license plates when about a dozen men walked out front from the rear of the home. Croswell called out to them but they ran, and Croswell immediately called in for reinforcements. Within minutes, police quickly set up a roadblock at the bottom of the lone road that led to the house to stop anyone from getting in, or out.

With more and more police arriving, some of the men scattered into the nearby woods, while others hopped into their cars and sped down the road, only to be stopped at the roadblock. When asked why they were at the house, nearly all said they were there to visit their sick friend Barbara. The police took the men into custody, including several who had been captured after fleeing into the woods. One by one they were identified, and when the police finished, they knew this was more than a sick call.

IT WAS JUST three weeks earlier, on October 25, 1957, when two men walked into a barbershop in New York City and shot Albert Anastasia to death.

Anastasia's long-simmering feud with Vito Genovese had finally reached a climax, as did Genovese's battle with Frank Costello, who months earlier avoided a similar fate after being shot and wounded as he walked out of his New York apartment. With Anastasia gone and Costello in hiding, it was time to quickly make amends. So Genovese called on Russell Bufalino to schedule a meeting of the Commission to make a peace.

The first call Bufalino made was to Stefano Magaddino. With the New York families on the verge of all-out war, Magaddino had the influence to gather everyone together, and they all agreed to meet at Barbara's country estate in Apalachin, New York.

By November 5, the meeting was set, and Barbara ordered nearly $500 worth of meat and cold cuts from a local store to be delivered to his home on November 13. Bufalino handled all the organizational duties, from notifying the guests and helping to arrange their transportation. A week before the meeting, Bufalino was in New York City making final arrangements with the heads of the New York families. He then left for Scranton, where he stayed at the Hotel Casey with several other men before driving up to Apalachin. Other attendees arrived by car or by plane, landing at the nearby Binghamton Airport.

When the meeting began, Genovese made his case to the Commission members, recounting his early years with Lucky Luciano, Anastasia and Costello and how he, Genovese, should have been given a leading position upon his return from Italy after World War II. His relative demotion was insulting, he said, and the insult festered for more than a decade. But now, with Anastasia dead and Costello agreeing to retirement, Genovese wanted the Commission's recognition as the new boss of what would be called the Genovese family, and a seat on the Commission.

Other business was up for discussion, including the garment industry, the Teamsters and narcotics. Earlier that year, in June, a struggle ensued between the warring factions for control of a portion of the New York City drug trade. One man, Frank Scalise, who had been associated with Lucky Luciano, was shot and killed in front of his Bronx home.

The men were in the middle of their discussions when Croswell and the state police happened upon the meeting, and the more than sixty gangsters in attendance fled.

Among the men arrested were Carlo Gambino, who assumed control of the Mangano family in New York that would eventually bear his name; Paul Castellano, a Gambino capo régime, or captain, who in later years would succeed Gambino but meet his end when an upstart named John Gotti plotted his execution in a hail of bullets in front of a New York steak house; John Scalish, the driver of the Cadillac registered to the Buckeye Cigarette

Service, and the head of the Cleveland mob; and Santo Trafficante Jr., the head of the South Florida family and majority owner of the Sans Souci casino in Havana. Trafficante was using a nom de plume, Louis Santos. Others in attendance included Stefano Magaddino; Sam Giancana, of Chicago; Nick Civella, of Kansas City; and representatives from families in Milwaukee, Dallas, Pittsburgh, Philadelphia, San Francisco and Los Angeles.

Also arrested were the Commission chairman, Joseph Bonanno, of New York, who was found by police hiding in a cornfield, and Vito Genovese, who tried to make his escape with Bufalino and several other men inside a 1957 Black Chrysler Imperial driven by Bufalino. The car, which was registered to the Medico Electric Company, was stopped at the roadblock at the end of the driveway.

Some sixty-four men were arrested, and the story made front-page news across the nation. A grand jury was convened on January 14, 1958, to determine if the men in attendance had broken any laws, and the ongoing investigation produced a treasure trove of intelligence.

They learned that Joseph Barbara, for instance, had business relationships dating back years with several men from Pittston and Detroit and maintained a ledger with debts due to a number of people. He owed $2,500 to Charles Bufalino; $10,000 to Louis Pagnotti, the owner of a Scranton coal company; $15,000 to Angelo Polizzi, the Detroit mobster; and $10,000 to Santo Volpe.

The official "Report on the Activities and Associations of Persons Identified as Present at the Residence of Joseph Barbara, Sr., at Apalachin, New York on November 14,

1957, and the Reasons for Their Presence," was submitted to New York governor W. Averell Harriman on April 23, 1958, and it concluded that the meeting had been planned in advance, was called to discuss mob business—most likely the murder of Anastasia—and that it had been organized by Russell Bufalino.

Apalachin was a milestone in the annals of organized crime, wiping out previous myths and misconceptions about the Italian Mafia, particularly the very public stance by the FBI that the Mafia even existed, and displayed once and for all the vast organizational network that connected family to family and city to city.

. Several mob factions seethed over what they believed to be a major breech. Bufalino escaped blame, but there were attempts on Stefano Magaddino's life, including an attempted bombing of his home. Aside from the embarrassment, the public for the first time now knew that, yes, there was an organized syndicate of mob families and, even worse, many of the men were now publicly identified.

The press that followed the astounding breakup of the national mob meeting followed the story for weeks, infuriating the Mafiosi and embarrassing the U.S. government, and the government wasted no time trying to prosecute several of the attendees, including Bufalino. On December 4, 1957, the FBI sent a telex reporting that the U.S. Immigration and Naturalization Service (INS) had begun investigating Bufalino's citizenship.

*INS, Philadelphia is conducting 'large scale' investigation of BUFALINO with view to deporting him. INS has information BUFALINO has claimed birth in Pittston, Pa. in 1903, though actually born in Italy. INS has located birth record Luzerne County, Pennsylvania which it believes forged, and through arrangements made by INS Washington, is taking record to Washington for examination by FBI laboratory. INS investigation now aimed at gathering all available information re foreign birth in preparation for interview of BUFALINO in near future.*

On December 16, 1957, the U.S. Immigration and Naturalization Service filed a motion of deportation against Bufalino, claiming, as the FBI reported, that he was not born in Pittston but in fact was born in Sicily. The deportation officer assigned to his case reported that the decision was based on a number of factors, including Bufalino's "failure to establish good moral character, his lying under oath regarding his birthplace and other false testimony and his two fraudulent entries into the United States in 1956."

Bufalino was ordered deported, but he appealed the decision, and he would find himself fighting the government for the next decade. Of more immediate concern was a subpoena to testify before the McClellan Senate Committee.

LED BY SENATOR John McClellan, of Arkansas, the Senate Select Committee on Improper Activities in Labor and Management was created before Apalachin to study organized crime's influence in labor racketeering. After Apalachin, the committee now had a road map and subpoenaed many of the gangsters that attended the meeting. The committee's chief counsel was Robert F. Kennedy, who would lead the questioning. Anticipating that nearly every gangster subpoenaed to testify before the committee would claim their Fifth Amendment rights, Kennedy used the sessions to show the world everything he could about the men, that they truly existed, controlled vast businesses and were nothing more than an organized group of hoods and criminals. His bitter confrontations with Jimmy Hoffa, one of 1,500 witnesses who would eventually testify, captured the nation's attention.

Unlike the bombastic Hoffa, who reveled in the back-and-forth with Kennedy, Bufalino had little to say. It didn't matter, since it was Kennedy who did all the talking.

*"The first witness this afternoon, Mr. Chairman, is Russell Bufalino," said Kennedy. "Would you tell me where you were born?"*

*"I respectfully decline to answer the question on the grounds it may tend to incriminate me," said Bufalino.*

*"Mr. Bufalino, our interest in you centers around your attending the meeting at Apalachin and also your union contacts. I think that we have some information that would indicate that you played a very prominent role in setting up the meeting at Apalachin; that you did it with the assistance of Mr. Barbara. I wonder if you would make any comments on that before we start to develop the facts that we have."*

*"I respectfully decline to answer the question on the ground that the question may tend to incriminate me."*

*"According to our information, you were born on October 29, 1903, in Montedoro, Italy. That is in Sicily. Is that correct?"*

*"I respectfully decline to answer the question on the ground that the question may tend to incriminate me."*

*"And yet despite that fact, the records at Luzerne County in Wilkes-Barre, Pa., show that you were born October 29, 1903, in Pittston Township, Pa."*

*"Is that a question?"*

*"Yes."*

*"I respectfully decline to answer that question on the grounds it may tend to incriminate me."*

*"Could you explain to the committee how it is that these records show that you were born in Pittston, Pa., when, in fact, you were born in Italy?"*

*"I respectfully decline to answer that question on the grounds that the question may tend to incriminate me."*

*"Is Mary Bufalino any relation to you?"*

*"I respectfully decline to answer the question on the grounds that the question may tend to incriminate me."*

*"Isn't it a fact that Mary Bufalino worked in the records office in Wilkes-Barre, Pa.?"*

*"I respectfully decline to answer the question on the grounds that the question may tend to incriminate me."*

*"Are you related to Mr. William Bufalino?"*

*"I respectfully decline to answer that question on the grounds that the question may tend to incriminate me."*

*"Isn't it correct that William Bufalino, who is*

*secretary-treasurer of Local 985 of the Teamsters, is a cousin of yours?"*

*"I respectfully decline to answer the question on the grounds that the question may tend to incriminate me."*

*"Isn't it correct also that Mr. William Bufalino is an attorney?"*

*"I respectfully decline to answer the question on the grounds that the question may tend to incriminate me."*

*"Did Mr. William Bufalino play any part in altering the records at the Wilkes-Barre Records Office?"*

*"I respectfully decline to answer the question on the grounds that the question may tend to incriminate me."*

*"Wasn't it the purpose of getting the records altered so that it would appear that you were born here in the United States, and, therefore, could not be deported to Italy?"*

*"I respectfully decline to answer the question on the grounds that the question may tend to incriminate me."*

*"Can you tell us what companies you own or operate in the Pittston–Wilkes-Barre–Scranton area?"*

*"I respectfully decline to answer the question on the grounds that the question may tend to incriminate me."*

*"Do you own and operate the Penn Drape & Curtain Co., of South Main Street, Pittston, Pa.?"*

*"I respectfully decline to answer the question on the grounds that the question may tend to incriminate me."*

*"Are the Sciandras of Pittston, Pa., in business with you?"*

*"I respectfully decline to answer the question on the grounds that the question may tend to degrade or incriminate me."*

"What was your wife's maiden name?"

"Carolina Sciandra."

"Isn't it a fact that Angelo Sciandra attended the meeting at Apalachin?"

"I respectfully decline to answer the question on the grounds that the question may tend to incriminate me."

"Could you tell us if you have ever been arrested, Mr. Bufalino?"

"I respectfully decline to answer the question on the grounds that the question may tend to incriminate me."

"Isn't it a fact that you have been arrested some seven or eight times?"

"I respectfully decline to answer the question on the grounds that the question may tend to incriminate me."

"And that you have not been convicted on any of those charges?"

"I respectfully decline to answer the question on the grounds that the question may tend to incriminate me."

"We have a number of companies with whom we believe you are connected, starting with the ABS Contracting Co., of Pittston, Pa. Is it correct that you are associated with them?"

"I respectfully decline to answer the question on the grounds that the question may tend to incriminate me."

"The Penn Drape & Curtain Co., in Pittston, Pa.?"

"The same answer."

"Would you answer the question."

"I respectfully decline to answer the question on the grounds that it may tend to incriminate me."

*"And you were associated with Bonnie Stewart, Inc., of New York City, N. Y.?"*

*"I respectfully decline to answer that question on the grounds it may tend to incriminate me."*

*"Isn't it correct that Dominic Alaimo and James Plumeri both had financial interests in that company also?"*

*"I respectfully decline to answer the question on the grounds it may tend to incriminate me."*

*"And Claudia Frocks of 224 West 35th Street, New York?"*

*"I respectfully decline to answer the question on the grounds that the question may tend to degrade or incriminate me."*

*"Isn't it correct that Angelo Sciandra also has an interest in that company?"*

*"I respectfully decline to answer that question on the grounds it may tend to incriminate me."*

*"And isn't it correct also that he pays you a certain amount of money each week for the work that you do for that company?"*

*"I respectfully decline to answer the question on the grounds it may tend to incriminate me."*

*"You are on the payroll as an expediter. Could you tell us what an expediter does?"*

*"I respectfully decline to answer the question on the grounds that the question may tend to incriminate me."*

*"Do you in fact do any work for this company, or are you on the payroll because of your connections, Mr. Bufalino?"*

"I respectfully decline to answer the question on the grounds it may tend to incriminate me."

"You receive from that company $105 a week gross, is that right?"

"I respectfully decline to answer the question on the grounds that the question may tend to incriminate me."

"And you were put on the payroll back in 1953, were you not?"

"I respectfully decline to answer the question on the grounds it may tend to incriminate me."

"Then also you are on the payroll of the Fair Frox as an expediter. You are on their payroll also?"

"I respectfully decline to answer the question on the grounds that the question may tend to incriminate me."

"That is F-a-i-r F-r-o-x, and you are on their payroll as expediter at $125 a week, are you not?"

"I respectfully decline to answer the question on the grounds it may tend to incriminate me."

"Could you tell us what you do to earn that money?"

"I respectfully decline to answer the question on the grounds it may tend to incriminate me."

"Isn't it a fact that part of the money you receive is to handle labor relations for those companies, and to prevent any trouble or difficulties with the union?"

"I respectfully decline to answer the question on the grounds that it may tend to incriminate me."

"Aren't you able to do that because of the contacts and associates that you have, Mr. Bufalino?"

"I respectfully decline to answer the question on the grounds that it may tend to incriminate me."

*"And they include such people, do they not, as Johnny Dioguardi?"*

*"I respectfully decline to answer the question on the grounds it may tend to incriminate me."*

*"John Ormento?"*

*"I respectfully decline to answer the question on the grounds it may tend to incriminate me."*

*"Nig Rosen?"*

*"I respectfully decline to answer the question on the grounds it may tend to incriminate me."*

*"Dominick Alaimo?"*

*"I respectfully decline to answer the question on the grounds it may tend to incriminate me."*

*"John Charles Montana?"*

*"I respectfully decline to answer the question on the grounds it may tend to incriminate me."*

*"Vito Genovese?"*

*"I respectfully decline to answer the question on the grounds it may tend to incriminate me."*

*"James A. Osticco?"*

*"I respectfully decline to answer the question on the grounds it may tend to incriminate me."*

*"Frank Carbo?"*

*"I respectfully decline to answer the question on the grounds it may tend to incriminate me."*

*"James Plumeri?"*

*"I respectfully decline to answer the question on the grounds it may tend to incriminate me."*

*"Thomas Lucchese?"*

"*I respectfully decline to answer the question on the grounds it may tend to incriminate me.*"

"*We have telephone calls from you, Mr. Bufalino, to L. G. Carriers, which is James Plumeri's company. Could you tell us what you discussed with them?*"

"*I respectfully decline to answer the question on the grounds it may tend to incriminate me.*"

"*What do you discuss with Charles Bufalino?*"

"*I respectfully decline to answer the question on the grounds that the question may tend to incriminate me.*"

"*The Tri-City Dress Co., owned by Anthony Guarnieri, can you tell us about that?*"

"*I respectfully decline to answer the question on the grounds that the question may tend to incriminate me.*"

"*The Vic Vera Sportswear Co., New York City, which is owned and operated by a close friend of James Plumeri?*"

"*I respectfully decline to answer the question on the grounds it may tend to incriminate me.*"

"*Isn't it a fact that James Plumeri set this lady up in the Vic Vera Sportswear Co.?*"

"*I respectfully decline to answer the question on the grounds it may tend to incriminate me.*"

"*And Harvic Sportswear, of Scranton, Pa. Can you tell us what you called them about?*"

"*I respectfully decline to answer the question on the grounds it may tend to incriminate me.*"

"*That is a shop, is it not, that is owned by Thomas Lucchese?*"

"*I respectfully decline to answer the question on the grounds it may tend to incriminate me.*"

"*Have you also had other sources of income from gambling, Mr. Bufalino?*"

"*I respectfully decline to answer the question on the grounds it may tend to incriminate me.*"

"*You have taken a great interest in basketball games, have you not?*"

"*I respectfully decline to answer the question on the grounds it may tend to incriminate me.*"

"*And when you go to New York, you stay at the Hotel Forrest in New York City, is that correct, Mr. Bufalino?*"

"*I respectfully decline to answer the question on the grounds that the question may tend to incriminate me.*"

"*Why is it that you and the individuals with police records very often stay at the Hotel Forrest in New York City?*"

"*I respectfully decline to answer the question on the grounds that the question may tend to incriminate me.*"

"*Isn't it correct that you arranged with Mr. Barbara to set up the meeting at Apalachin in November 1957?*"

"*I respectfully decline to answer the question on the grounds it may tend to incriminate me.*"

"*Isn't it correct that you were talking by telephone with Mr. Barbara frequently just prior to the meeting at Apalachin?*"

"*I respectfully decline to answer the question on the grounds it may tend to incriminate me.*"

"*According to the information that we have, you made long distance telephone calls to Barbara on June 8,*"

11, 23, two on the 28th, July 23, July 27, September 4, September 11, September 12, October 6, October 13, and October 26, is that correct?"

"I respectfully decline to answer the question on the grounds that the question may tend to incriminate me."

"And he called you on June 5, 10, 24, July 20, August 9, and October 23?"

"I respectfully decline to answer the question on the grounds it may tend to incriminate me."

"And isn't it correct that you in fact made hotel reservations for some of these individuals attending the meeting at Apalachin?"

"I respectfully decline to answer the question on the grounds it may tend to incriminate me."

"Isn't it a fact that you made a hotel reservation at the Casey Hotel in Scranton, Pennsylvania, for November 13, 1957?"

"I respectfully decline to answer the question on the grounds it may tend to incriminate me."

"And you made hotel reservations for an individual by the name of J. Cerrito, of Los Gatos, California?"

"I respectfully decline to answer the question on the grounds it may tend to incriminate me."

"And that another reservation for the same night was made for J. Civello of Dallas, Texas?"

"I respectfully decline to answer the question on the grounds it may tend to incriminate me."

"And this individual did, in fact, attend the meeting at Apalachin, is that correct?"

"*I respectfully decline to answer the question on the grounds it may tend to incriminate me.*"

"*And Scozzari, from San Gabriel, California?*"

"*I respectfully decline to answer the question on the grounds it may tend to incriminate me.*"

"*While he was there, Mr. Scozzari put in two telephone calls to you, isn't that correct?*"

"*I respectfully decline to answer the question on the grounds it may tend to incriminate me.*"

"*And isn't it a fact that Mr. Scozzari attended the meeting at Apalachin?*"

"*I respectfully decline to answer the question on the grounds it may tend to incriminate me.*"

"*And Frank DeSimone, you also made a reservation for him.*"

"*I respectfully decline to answer the question on the grounds it may tend to incriminate me.*"

"*Mr. Scozzari, when he was arrested, or stopped by the police, had $10,000 on him, but listed himself as unemployed. Can you give us any explanation for that?*"

"*I respectfully decline to answer the question on the grounds it may tend to incriminate me.*"

"*All these hotel reservations that were made for these 5 individuals, of which we can show that 3 actually attended the meeting in Apalachin, were all charged to you personally, isn't that correct, Mr. Bufalino?*"

"*I respectfully decline to answer the question on the grounds it may tend to incriminate me.*"

"Did these other two individuals, Lanza and Scozzari, attend the meeting but were not caught?"

"I respectfully decline to answer the question on the grounds it may tend to incriminate me."

"When you came to the meeting, you came, did you not, with DeSimone, Civello and Scozzari?"

"I respectfully decline to answer the question on the grounds it may tend to incriminate me."

"That automobile that you drove was owned by William Medico, was it not?"

"I respectfully decline to answer the question on the grounds it may tend to incriminate me."

"And he owns the Medico Electric Motor Company in Pittsburgh, Pennsylvania?"

"I respectfully decline to answer the question on the grounds it may tend to incriminate me."

"Excuse me. That should be in Pittston, Pennsylvania. He owns the Medico Electric Motor Company. in Pittston, does he not?"

"I respectfully decline to answer the question on the grounds it may tend to incriminate me."

"This is the same individual that Mr. Montana stated that he was driving down to see, to find out how his compressor was coming?"

"I respectfully decline to answer the question on the grounds it may tend to incriminate me."

"And you in fact were driving an automobile belonging to one of his companies up to the meeting at Apalachin, were you not?"

"*I respectfully decline to answer the question on the grounds it may tend to incriminate me.*"

"*At the time that the New York State troopers checked your car, you had Vito Genovese with you, did you not?*"

"*I respectfully decline to answer the question on the grounds it may tend to incriminate me.*"

"*Gerardo Cateno?*"

"*I respectfully decline to answer the question on the grounds it may tend to incriminate me.*"

"*Dominick Olivetto?*"

"*I respectfully decline to answer the question on the grounds it may tend to incriminate me.*"

"*And Joseph Ida?*"

"*I respectfully decline to answer the question on the grounds it may tend to incriminate me.*"

"*And you stayed, when you were in Binghamton in March—you made another visit to Joseph Barbara in March 1957, did you not, Mr. Bufalino?*"

"*I respectfully decline to answer on the grounds it may tend to incriminate me.*"

"*And at that time, you were with Vincenzo Osticco, isn't that right?*"

"*I respectfully decline to answer the question on the grounds it may tend to incriminate me.*"

"*And also with you was Angelo Sciandra, and you stayed at the Arlington Hotel, in Binghamton, New York?*"

"*I respectfully decline to answer the question on the grounds it may tend to incriminate me.*"

"And the bill was charged to the Canada Dry Beverage Company, of Endicott, New York, was it not?"

"I respectfully decline to answer the question on the grounds it may tend to incriminate me."

"What were you there for? What business were you there on?"

"I respectfully decline to answer the question on the grounds it may tend to incriminate me."

"Do you know how your cousin, William Bufalino, was made head of Local 985 of the Teamsters?"

"I respectfully decline to answer the question on the grounds it may tend to incriminate me."

"Do you know Mr. James Hoffa?"

"I respectfully decline to answer the question on the grounds it may tend to incriminate me."

"Do you know Mr. Santo Volpe, from Pennsylvania?"

"I respectfully decline to answer the question on the grounds it may tend to incriminate me."

Kennedy paused after the long series of questions, then turned to Senator McClellan.

"Mr. Chairman," said Kennedy. "We consider that this individual is a very important figure. He has a number of the dress companies that operate in Pennsylvania. He also played an important role in the labor negotiations that took place at the beginning of this year. He is a close associate of Mr. Chait and it would appear that he was the one, together with Barbara, who set up and made the *appointments and arrangements for setting up the meeting at Apalachin. He is a man of considerable importance and a man of great contacts throughout the United States and the underworld."*

*"Do you want to comment upon those statements?" said McClellan.*

*"I respectfully decline to answer the question on the grounds it may tend to incriminate me," said Bufalino.*

# NINE

When Jimmy Hoffa was elected president of the International Brotherhood of Teamsters in 1957, it capped a remarkable career that had begun twenty years earlier in Detroit.

Hoffa had been the Teamsters national vice president since 1952, serving under then president Dave Beck, who had been accused of stealing from the Teamsters by failing to repay a $300,000 loan. When he was questioned about the loan during his testimony before the McClellan Committee, Beck invoked his Fifth Amendment right more than one hundred times. The negative publicity that followed his testimony led Beck to decline another run for the Teamster presidency, and Hoffa stepped in and gained the votes at the Teamster convention in Miami Beach to become their new leader.

Hoffa now headed the most powerful union in the

country, and given his long-rumored associations to organized crime figures in Detroit and New York, he drew
greater scrutiny in his new position, especially from the
McClellan Committee and its zealous chief counsel, Robert F. Kennedy.

Kennedy was relentless in his pursuit to expose Teamster
corruption, particularly Hoffa's alleged relationships with
organized crime. During his testimony before the committee, Hoffa in turn was pugnacious, giving purposely vague
answers while going head-to-head with Kennedy during
televised hearings that transfixed the nation.

The government wasted no time prosecuting Hoffa,
who was eventually indicted in December 1957 for ille-
gally bugging Teamster offices to determine if any of his
people were sharing information with the McClellan
Committee. The trial ended in a hung jury, with one lone
holdout for conviction. A second trial was interrupted
when a juror reportedly was approached with a bribe to
acquit Hoffa. That juror was replaced, and when the trial
ended, Jimmy Hoffa was acquitted.

The failed prosecution only served to embolden Hoffa,
who by now considered himself one of the most powerful
men in the country. Despite his standing, Hoffa knew he
still needed friends, especially those with unique skills
who could be tasked with special assignments.


FRANK SHEERAN'S INTRODUCTION to Jimmy Hoffa
was on the telephone.

Sheeran was a U.S. Army veteran who served as a rifle-

Russell Bufalino, circa 1955. Bufalino claimed ownership of casinos in Havana and clothing manufacturing facilities in New York and Pennsylvania, and he also exerted great influence over the Teamsters union and its rich Central States pension fund. Bufalino was a major target of the FBI's "Top Hoodlum Program" and, according to a 1964 United States Senate subcommittee, was "one of the most ruthless and powerful leaders of the Mafia in the United States."

Bufalino, Angelo Sciandra and James Osticco (left to right) outside federal court in New York in May 1959 to answer charges relating to the infamous mob meeting in Apalachin, New York. It was Bufalino who organized the November 1957 gathering to help his friend Vito Genovese make peace following the murder of Albert Anastasia and the shooting of Frank Costello.

U. S. Representative Daniel Flood (D-PA) enjoyed a close relationship with Russell Bufalino from the 1950s until he was forced to resign in 1980.

Bufalino's underboss James Osticco, who attended the 1957 Apalachin meeting with Bufalino, was convicted of obstruction of justice in 1983 for tampering with the Louis DeNaples' jury.

Louis DeNaples with the Rev. Joseph Sica (right). A curious sight, Sica was at DeNaples' side throughout the application process for a casino license. Both men were charged in 2008 with lying to the Pennsylvania Gaming Control Board about their past ties with Russell Bufalino.

Rev. Sica (left) once claimed debts of nearly $250,000, with over $100,000 owed to a bank controlled by DeNaples (right).

Pennsylvania State Police commissioner Jeffrey Miller (left) and deputy commissioner Ralph Periandi (right). After the Rendell administration shut the police out of the gaming initiative, Periandi began a secret "Black Ops" investigation that ultimately led to a grand jury and charges against Louis DeNaples and Rev. Sica. PHOTO COURTESY OF THE POCONO RECORD

Former Pennsylvania governor Ed Rendell and members of his administration were the original targets of the state police gaming investigation, but interference by the state Supreme Court in the DeNaples case stymied the probe.

PHOTO COURTESY OF THE POCONO RECORD

William D'Elia (above) testifying before the Pennsylvania Crime Commission circa 1982. D'Elia rose from Russell Bufalino's driver to the head of the crime family following Bufalino's death in 1994. Following his arrest in 2006 for trying to kill a witness, D'Elia (below) agreed to cooperate with federal and state prosecutors and told the grand jury investigating Louis DeNaples that he and DeNaples had a personal and business relationship that spanned more than thirty years.

By 1975 Russell Bufalino was at the height of his power. After beating back the government's attempts to deport him, he took over leadership of Buffalo's Magaddino family and assumed temporary control over New York's Genovese family. Combined with his influence within the Teamsters union, Bufalino was arguably one of the most powerful mobsters in the nation. But then came the *Time* magazine article, which identified Bufalino as one of the mobsters recruited by the CIA in its plots to depose Fidel Castro. Just weeks later, Jimmy Hoffa disappeared.

man with the Forty-Fifth Infantry Division in Europe during World War II. Known as the "Thunderbird Division," the Forty-Fifth had spent an incredible 511 days in combat, and Sheeran was on the front lines for more than 400 of those bloody days. Serving under General George Patton, the division was trained to kill with no remorse, which it did from the day it landed in Sicily in 1943. Soon known as the "Killer Division," Sheeran couldn't count the number of Germans and Italians whose lives he had ended. Despite a casualty rate that reached near 100 percent, Sheeran somehow survived his 411 days on the front lines, but the war left him emotionally detached. Killing became easy, and it was a talent that would be found useful a decade after his return to America.

It was in central New York State where Sheeran first met Russell Bufalino. Sheeran was working for a food company in Philadelphia and driving a truck through the Binghamton, New York, area when the engine sputtered. He pulled into a truck stop to take a look and was approached by an older man with a tool kit. It was Bufalino, who explained that in his younger days he had been trained as a mechanic. Sheeran had no idea who Bufalino was, or that the "chance" meeting may not have been by chance at all.

Aside from driving a truck, Sheeran had been doing odd jobs on the side to make extra money, from selling football lottery tickets to picking up payments for a local Philadelphia loan shark. Word eventually filtered to Bufalino about a hungry, six feet four U.S. Army vet who had spent more than a year on the front lines. It wasn't long after they met at the truck stop that Sheeran and Bufalino saw each other again, at a restaurant in Philadelphia.

Bufalino was sitting with Angelo Bruno when he saw the big Irishman standing out above the patrons at the bar. Bufalino sent an underling to bring Sheeran to his table and greeted him warmly. Their reintroduction eventually led to a job, with Sheeran serving as a driver for Bufalino, chauffeuring him to business meetings throughout the northeast. But Bufalino wasn't just interested in Sheeran's driving ability. It was only a matter of time before Sheeran proved his true value when he accepted a job to kill a low-level gangster. Bufalino had relied on a handful of men to dispatch enemies and others whose business interests interfered with his. Chief among Bufalino's killers was Gioacchino "Dandy Jack" Parisi, otherwise known as Jack, who had worked with Albert Anastasia in New York as a member of the infamous "Murder Incorporated" crew of mob killers before fleeing to Hazleton in the 1930s to avoid a murder indictment.

Killing was still easy for Sheeran. No feeling. No remorse. The order from Bufalino would usually come with little advance notice, maybe a day or so, and Sheeran would carry out the job using a gun, a knife, even his bare hands, and dispose of the remains. After cementing his relationship with Bufalino, Sheeran shared his wish for a bigger role with the Teamsters. Sheeran had been a member of Local 107 in Philadelphia since 1947, and Bufalino subsequently put him in touch with Hoffa, who, like Bufalino, had use for Sheeran's talents. Within a year, Sheeran was working for Hoffa's home Teamsters Local

299 in Detroit, while Bufalino would be focusing his attention on events outside the United States.

ON JANUARY 1, 1959, Fulgencio Batista fled Cuba ahead of the quickly advancing rebel army led by Fidel Castro. It was Batista, believing his power was absolute and unquestioned, who ordered the release of Castro from prison in 1955 following the failed attack of a Cuban army barracks in 1953. The young revolutionary, a lawyer by trade, went to Mexico with Che Guevara to plot the revolution that would ultimately lead to Castro's overthrow of the Batista dictatorship. A short time after forcing Batista to flee, Castro nationalized the hotels and casinos and threw the mobsters off the island.

Bufalino's flight from Cuba was on a boat with Vincent Alo, a member of the Genovese family who had for years been one of Meyer Lansky's top lieutenants and partners in the casino business.

Lansky and Bufalino first met in the 1930s, when Lansky partnered with Lucky Luciano in various gambling endeavors in Florida and Cuba. Lansky had also supported Bugsy Siegel's efforts to create a gambling mecca in a sandy outpost known as Las Vegas. But Lansky directed his full attention to Cuba, and it was Lansky who set the initial terms with Batista that led to the explosion of new casinos in Havana in the 1950s.

It was through Lansky that Bufalino got his good friend Kelly Mannarino of Pittsburgh a piece of the Sans Souci casino following discussions at Bufalino's Gold

Coast Lounge in Hollywood, Florida, where he often met with south Florida boss Santo Trafficante and New Orleans boss Carlos Marcello.

But as the changing political climate took hold during the late 1950s, the chief concern, aside from the McClellan Committee, was what to do about Cuba. The island was far too lucrative, and it was producing revenues from a variety of businesses, not just the casinos, that simply could not be lost. Organized crime had long supported Batista, though that support had been waning, given Batista's constant demands for bigger slices of their casino deals.

The solution was to play both sides of the Cuban problem and quietly support Castro along with Batista. As the revolution grew, the Mafiosi provided each side arms shipments after Castro agreed that if he indeed prevailed, his new supporters would keep their casinos and other businesses.

But after arriving in Havana on January 8, 1959, Castro didn't waste any time tossing the mob bosses and their underlings off the island. Lansky and Bufalino beat him to it, fleeing the island in boats just days before. The casinos were subsequently nationalized, and Castro outlawed gambling as he quickly drifted the country away from the influence of the United States and toward its nemesis, the Soviet Union. Bufalino, along with the other Mafiosi who stood to lose millions from the events in Cuba, was irate, and regaining control of the island was a priority, even an obsession. A year later, in 1960, it appeared that the answer to everyone's prayers was the newly elected president, an Irish Catholic senator from Massachusetts.

It was before the November 1960 election when Bufalino received a call from Jimmy Hoffa. The two men needed to talk, only not over the phone, said Hoffa. The Teamsters had left Indianapolis and built a palatial headquarters in Washington, D.C., and when Bufalino arrived, Hoffa said he had been contacted by the U.S. Central Intelligence Agency, and the agency wanted to do something about Fidel Castro.

Bufalino, along with the other mob leaders, had no use for any government organization. The FBI and Department of Immigration had hounded them in recent years, as did the various congressional committees. But the CIA was a different animal. Formed after World War II to provide the government with international intelligence through the use of covert operatives placed in countries around the world, the CIA was a civilian agency that operated with little government oversight. During the years following World War II, the CIA morphed into a rogue entity. And following Castro's takeover of Cuba and his alliance with the Soviet Union, the CIA quickly deduced that Castro had to be eliminated. How to do it was up for debate. The idea on the table that drew lukewarm support was to enlist some of the gangsters who lost their lucrative interests in Cuba. The idea somehow made sense, given the Mafiosi were angry and motivated, and if any word of their effort was publicized it would be easy for the CIA to deny any allegations that the agency was involved. After all, who would believe that a highly respected government entity would associate with organized crime figures?

It was Hoffa who would serve as the go-between. Hoffa had friends like Bufalino who didn't just lose casinos and other businesses in Havana—they left behind fortunes. And in Bufalino's case, there was also the nearly $1 million in cash he buried in the ground hours before fleeing the island. The deal, said Hoffa, was simple: the CIA offered to help Bufalino retrieve the money if he in return would help in eliminating Castro and/or provide logistics in the event an invading army reached Cuba.

Hoffa told Bufalino that he had already reached out to Sam Giancana in Chicago and Johnny Roselli in Los Angeles to gain their cooperation, and all were led to believe that the plan had been approved by the newly elected president, John F. Kennedy. Cooperating with the Kennedy administration through the CIA seemed a sure bet to return control of the casinos to their rightful owners, and all agreed it was a deal they couldn't pass up. There was also a belief, at least by Hoffa, that helping the CIA might help in getting the Justice Department off his back. Besides, word had filtered of an arrangement Kennedy had with Giancana or, rather, a deal struck by Kennedy's wealthy father, Joseph, that had turned the election in Kennedy's favor, so a precedent had been set for some level of cooperation.

By April 1961, Bufalino confided to a few close friends that Kennedy was planning something for Cuba. In a telex dated April 12, 1961, two FBI agents reported that Russell Bufalino had arrived in Washington, D.C., supposedly to meet with his attorneys handling his ongoing deportation case. Bufalino was still under surveillance as part of the FBI's Top Hoodlum Program, and the telex aroused little concern. Bufalino slipped out of Washington and headed to Florida and then to the Bahamas, where he boarded a boat and waited for transport to Cuba.

# TEN

The disastrous outcome of the Bay of Pigs invasion and the loss of Cuba were monumental blows to the gangsters who had profited for years from the island, and their anger toward the Kennedy administration was of such intensity that the only way to make them whole would be the unthinkable.

The conversations began immediately after the failed invasion and were further fueled when Bufalino and others finally returned home. They had, as a group, been disrespected to such a degree that under normal circumstances, the offending party would have been dispatched immediately and with extreme prejudice.

They may have been at their cores violent hoods, but many, including Bufalino and Meyer Lansky, had always been known as men of their word. It was their bond, and no one ever doubted them when they said or promised something. How to deal with the president of the United States and his troublesome brother, who was now attorney general, was a matter that would take some consideration.

As they pondered and spoke secretly of their options, the U.S. Department of Justice began placing more resources and men into its ongoing Top Hoodlum Program. Only now everyone knew they weren't just hoodlums, but members of a secretive, violent national organization that had a firm grip on several major U.S. industries, from the shipping docks on the East and West Coasts to the garment industry and the Teamsters union, which controlled interstate trucking.

Beginning in 1961, the new efforts by the FBI, under the orders of its new attorney general, Robert F. Kennedy, would be to crush organized crime wherever and whenever it could. To meet that end, Kennedy ordered the FBI to begin daily surveillance of every mob boss in the nation, and that included Russell Bufalino.

Agents began a virtual twenty-four-hour watch on Bufalino, with reports filed to the Philadelphia bureau every Monday, Wednesday and Friday. The regular surveillance began in March 1961, and one of the first texts from the Philadelphia bureau to J. Edgar Hoover provided a bombshell piece of information: Russell Bufalino was sending arms to Cuba.

The information came from an informant who knew Paul Winter, an anti-Communist who in 1938 had stolen records from the Wilkes-Barre office of the Communist Party. Winter subsequently copied the documents and distributed them to local organizations and thus identified the Communist Party members to the public. The FBI was amused by Winter, chiefly for his interest in outing Communists, and remained in touch with him.

According to the FBI text, the informant reported that he was with Winter in February 1961, and Winter revealed that Bufalino was working for a secret organization that was manufacturing and shipping arms to Cuba to use against Fidel Castro. Unbeknownst to the FBI, the "secret" organization was the CIA. But the FBI decided against pursuing the matter, saying it was out of their jurisdiction and a matter for the Department of Customs.

The bureau did take an interest in other matters, particularly Bufalino's hangouts and acquaintances. Among his favorite haunts were Club 82, in Pittston; Preno's Restaurant and the Sahara Bar, in Scranton; and Medico Industries, formerly Medico Electric Company, now receiving an increasing share of U.S. government contracts.

During Bufalino's visits to New York, he'd usually stay in his suite at the Forrester Hotel, which was paid for by Monet Fashions Incorporated, a company in which he had an interest. Among those often accompanying Bufalino were the closest members of his Pennsylvania crew. Anthony Guarnieri, a capo régime whose interest was in the drug trades; Casper "Cappy" Giumento, one of Bufalino's closest confidantes and his Everyman, who served a variety of duties, from chauffeuring Bufalino to meetings to picking up envelopes filled with cash from people in business with Bufalino; Al Baldassari, an associate who ran Bufalino's gaming operations and was identified as a Scranton hoodlum by the Kefauver Committee; and

James Plumeri, another close associate, who went by the name of Jimmy Doyle and got his start working in the 1930s for Lucky Luciano before joining the Bufalino family.

The FBI also watched closely as Bufalino spent hours at the Vesuvio restaurant holding court with New York gangsters, who, in a surprising turn, appeared to be paying their respects to Bufalino.

Back in Pennsylvania, Bufalino had displayed a keen ability to stay out of trouble. And when he was charged with something, he had the clout to quash it. When he arrived at the Luzerne County courthouse to answer to a speeding violation in September 1961, Bufalino shook hands with members of the Forty Fort police department, which gave him the ticket. The county judge even went as far as to visit the spot of the alleged violation before dismissing the charge completely.

Aside from their routine reports of his associations and business affairs, the FBI agents noted that Bufalino liked to deal in cash and kept little in a checking account he shared with his wife, Carrie, at the First National Community Bank, usually no more than $300. The FBI also noted that Bufalino was a big sports fan, especially when it came to boxing. Bufalino had begun managing boxers and even promoted fights with Al Flora, an ex-boxer from Baltimore.

Perhaps most interesting to the FBI were Bufalino's paramours. Though married for more than thirty years, Bufalino always maintained liaisons with several girlfriends in different cities. One of his most recent flames was Jane Collins, a wealthy divorcée who lived with a prostitute, Judy McCarthy. The FBI reported that Collins and Bufalino would use McCarthy's apartment to rendezvous whenever McCarthy was out of town. Bufalino had been seeing Collins for more than a year after he first spotted her at a local textile company. Instead of introducing himself, he had a mutual friend phone Collins with a tip on a horse race. Hearing that it was a sure thing, Collins made a bet and won $100. The following week, she received another tip on another race and won $250. A third tip netted $1,000. Because of the large amount, the money had to be delivered by Bufalino himself.

Bufalino's interest in Collins didn't just come from her good looks. He told close associates that the loss of his Cuban interests and the cost of fighting the government over his deportation proceedings decimated his finances, and his friends took up collections to pay his attorney's fees. Collins, on the other hand, wasn't hurting for money. In fact, she escaped her marriage as the co-owner of the Wyoming Coal Company. As the FBI described her, she was the type of woman Bufalino needed at this point in his life. Bufalino wasn't broke by any stretch of the imagination, but he was cunning enough to give the appearance that he was hurting financially.

Once they started seeing each other, Collins began paying Bufalino's bills. She even bought him a Cadillac for his birthday. Bufalino, in turn, used his Communist-hating friend Paul Winter to spy on Collins' ex-husband, Frank.

Bufalino's supposedly poor financial status seemed to

improve dramatically whenever he left the Scranton area. On his trips to Philadelphia, the FBI noted he'd visit with friends at the Penn Center Social Club. A choreographer there, Kay Carlton, provided prostitutes for Bufalino, for which he paid the women $600 to $800 each.

Unbeknownst to Collins, Bufalino had another girlfriend, a barmaid named Alberta Stocker. And it was his relationship with Stocker where the FBI believed it had an opening.

IN THE SIX years since Apalachin, Russell Bufalino battled the U.S. government relentlessly to stay in the United States.

The deportation saga had been a drain on his finances and his emotions after he was first ordered in 1958 to leave the country for lying about his citizenship, his illegal entrée into the country from the Bahamas in 1956 and his failure to establish he had good moral character. On two occasions, he was certain he'd be forced out of the country, and he went to New York to plan for his departure.

But Bufalino had hired famed immigration attorney Jack Wasserman, who did everything he could to delay the case and keep Bufalino in the country. Wasserman represented Carlos Marcello, the New Orleans crime boss, during his deportation battle with the government, delaying the government more than a decade. Initially probed by the Kefauver Committee, the government began Marcello's deportation proceedings in 1952, but Wasserman appealed the case all the way to the U.S. Supreme Court, which ultimately ruled against him. In 1955, Wasserman argued that Marcello was not an Italian citizen and sought an injunction from the Italian courts preventing Marcello from being deported there. Marcello was sent to Guatemala in 1959, but Wasserman fought the order and Marcello was returned to New Orleans, where to the government's great embarrassment he remained.

Bufalino's case was somewhat simpler and clear-cut after it was determined that someone inside the Luzerne County Clerks Office had changed the recording of Bufalino's place of birth in the county ledger. The perpetrator simply erased "Montedoro, Sicily" and replaced it with "Pittston, Pa."

He was ordered "deportable" in April 1958 but appealed the decision, and the case was remanded until September 1958, when the appeal was dismissed. A petition for review was filed, but that too was dismissed, in April 1959. The U.S. Court of Appeals issued a grant of summary judgment in April 1960 ordering Bufalino to leave the country. Bufalino filed yet another appeal, claiming he was the victim of prejudgment by the U.S. Immigration and Naturalization Service, and he would remain in the United States awaiting a decision but for how long was anyone's guess. With the deportation case now on hold, Bufalino could put his attention to other matters at hand, one of which would require his absolute attention.

In September 1963, the FBI picked up information that Bufalino had been communicating with someone in Mexico. The first calls came from Guadalajara, and then, in November, several other calls originated from Mexico

City. It was around the same time, unbeknownst to the FBI, that Frank Sheeran received a call from Jimmy Hoffa, who directed him to visit Bufalino at his Kingston, Pennsylvania, home. When Sheeran arrived, he was told by Bufalino to see their friends in Brooklyn, pick up a package and drive it to Baltimore. The "friends" were members of the Genovese family, including a captain named Tony Provenzano who also ran a New Jersey Teamster local. When Sheeran arrived, Provenzano handed him a duffel bag with directions to meet a pilot in Baltimore. Sheeran didn't look inside the bag, but, having carried guns before, he quickly deduced he was carrying three rifles. He drove to Baltimore, made his delivery and returned to Pennsylvania. Just a few days later, President John F. Kennedy was assassinated. Sheeran was convinced that the rifles he delivered were used in the shooting, and he couldn't help but notice that Bufalino was in good spirits when he met up with him at the Vesuvio restaurant a week after the murder.

# ELEVEN

The U.S. Department of Justice had tried for seven years to put away Jimmy Hoffa. Four times he had been charged with various crimes, and each time he walked away. But in March 1964, a federal jury in Chattanooga, Tennessee, convicted Hoffa of jury tampering. Four months later, he was convicted of fraud in another trial, in Chicago, for improperly using the Teamsters pension fund. Combined, he was facing up to thirteen years in prison.

The March trial in Tennessee was, like Hoffa's other battles with federal prosecutors, a circus and stemmed from his 1962 mistrial on conspiracy charges. In this case, prosecutors were able to convince a fifth jury that Hoffa and others tried to bribe two jurors in the 1962 trial.

Hoffa claimed he had been railroaded and promised to appeal, but it was clear that his imprisonment was only a matter of time. So in December 1964, a meeting was scheduled at the suburban Detroit home of William Bufalino to discuss the future of the Teamsters and, more important, the use of the Central States pension fund. Russell Bufalino flew from Scranton to Detroit under an assumed name and drove to his cousin William's home. There he would meet with Joseph Barbara Jr., Michael Polizzi and Vincent and Frank Meli. The conversation focused on the Teamsters and Hoffa's pending prison sentence.

The FBI knew about the meeting. Bufalino was still under their watch, though curiously there were no FBI reports between November 1963 and early January 1964. The telexes resumed in late January 1964. One reported that Bufalino was interested in supporting a county judge, Sydney Hoffman, who was running for superior judge. Another telex reported a meeting between Bufalino and his friend, a businessman named Joseph Sica, and two other men, who had traveled to Pittsburgh to discuss a Teamster loan for a shopping center there.

In October 1964, yet another telex described how Bufalino sought to mend his relationship with Jane Collins with tickets to Yankee Stadium in New York to see the Yankees play the St. Louis Cardinals in the World Series. They'd had a falling out a year earlier, and Collins took up with another man. Furious, Bufalino sought to end that relationship, but every time he visited with Collins, their conversations would end with Bufalino yelling and stomping away. When he showed up to offer the Yankee tickets, he also complained about a new federal brief in his deportation case. The government was now alleging that he was two years old when he arrived in the United States in 1903 when in fact he was two months old. But Collins didn't want to hear any more about his lengthy and bitter case, and she didn't want to go with him to New York or anywhere else for that matter. Bufalino left with the tickets in hand.

Unbeknownst to Bufalino, Collins was talking to the FBI, which was assisting the immigration department in its ongoing battle to deport Bufalino. Five months later, in March 1965, Bufalino's petition to set aside his original deportation order from 1958 was denied, and he was ordered deported to Brazil. The decision in large part was based on the testimony of Collins, whom the FBI credited with furnishing "considerable information."

Like he did before, Bufalino appealed the decision, and his deportation was once again deferred pending another court hearing.

*ASSOCIATED PRESS*
Oct. 28, 1969

*A Pennsylvania manufacturing firm linked to the Mafia by a Senate subcommittee has won millions of dollars in defense contracts from the Pentagon. Medico Industries Inc. of Pittston, Pa., currently is working on a $4 million contract to produce parts for rocket warheads used extensively in Vietnam. Since 1966, the firm has received about $12 million in Army, Navy, and Air Force con-*

tracts. *Pentagon records indicate it has performed well on all its defense work.*

*Medico Industries' present contracts do not involve classified material. However, a Pentagon spokesman said the firm and its principal officers had a security clearance from Jan. 28, 1968 to June 20, 1968. It was terminated at the company's request—a request which Pentagon sources said came after security officials asked for additional information about its officers.*

*The company's name has cropped up in the organized crime investigations of a Senate subcommittee headed by Sen. John L. McClellan, D Ark. In 1964, McClellan's subcommittee listed Medico Electric Motor Co., later to become known as Medico Industries, as a principal hangout of Russell Bufalino, whom it described as "one of the most ruthless and powerful leaders of the Mafia in the United States."*

*William Medico, former president and now general manager of Medico Industries, was listed in the same report as among the "criminal associates" of Bufalino.*

*James A. Osticco, the firm's traffic manager, was present in 1957 when New York State Police broke up the Apalachin Conference—a meeting of top Mafia figures from throughout the United States. The participants also included Bufalino and Vito Genovese, once described as "king of the rackets."*

*Bufalino has been battling deportation since 1952. According to the McClellan committee's 1964 report, the Sicilian-born Mafia leader has been active in narcotics trafficking, labor racketeering, and dealing in stolen jewels and furs. Last year, Bufalino was charged with transporting stolen television sets across state lines.*

*Investigators say Bufalino and Medico have been friends since Bufalino moved to Pittston from Buffalo, N.Y., in 1938. A confidential report in the files of state and federal law enforcement officials refers to a company listed in the Senate report as being owned by Bufalino and says: "One of the silent partners in this enterprise is said to be William Medico . . . who is believed to have money invested in a number of places where the subject (Bufalino) acts as front man."*

*In a telephone interview, Medico said he has no business interests with Bufalino. He said he has known Bufalino all his life.*

*As for the McClellan committee report that Bufalino frequents the Medico plant, Medico said, "Sure he comes to see us. We're selling him equipment; he's a customer. I can't tell him to get the hell out."*

*The firm's record of getting government contracts goes back to the 1950s. It has produced such items as maintenance platforms for the Air Force and Navy, rebuilt generators for the Signal Corps, rebuilt machine tools and hydraulic wing jacks for the Army, Navy and Air Force. It also has had contracts from the cities of New York and Detroit.*

*In 1963 it competed with eight other firms to take over management of a government-ammunition plant in Scranton, Pa., but lost out to a lower bidder.*

*In 1968 Medico Industries was one of the 166 compa-*

*nies from which the Army sought bids to produce parts
for 2.75-inch rocket warheads. Ten firms, including
Medico, responded and six got contracts. Medico was not
among them.*

*But in the summer of 1968, the Army announced it
needed still more warheads to fill Vietnam requirements.
The four unsuccessful bidders on the earlier round were
invited to bid again. All four, including Medico, got
contracts. The Medico contract, awarded September 19,
1968, called for supply of 510,000 parts for $3,090,600.*

*Then, in December 1968, Medico was among the pro-
ducers invited to submit proposals for shifting to production of a different and costlier type 2.75-inch warhead.
The firm received a contract on Dec. 31 to supply 380,000
parts at a cost of $4,012,800. That contract is still in
effect.*

*Under Defense Department regulations, a company
can not be cleared for work on classified projects until its
key personnel are given a National Agency check. This
includes a search of FBI name and fingerprint files.*

*If any derogatory information is found, it is up to the
Defense Industrial Security Command at Columbus,
Ohio, to determine if it is serious enough to warrant further investigation. If such a determination is made the
case is referred to a higher level for review. No such reference was made when Medico's application was processed.*

*In addition to security checks, all prospective defense
contractors also undergo a pre-award review to determine their ability to produce. The personal background
of company officials is not a factor in such reviews.*

*Medico Industries' success in obtaining government contracts has helped it expand from a small electrical company housed in a former mule barn to a large modern plant on the outskirts of Pittston. With a work force of about 400 during peak contract periods, the firm is one of the largest employers in the coal mining area.*

*William Medico and his four brothers, all officers in the family firm, are often in the news as participants in civic affairs, charity drives and occasionally politics, in the city of 13,000 midway between Scranton and Wilkes-Barre.*

THE STORY THAT ran in newspapers across the country about Medico Industries was a thorough account of its business dealings, dubious and otherwise, but it didn't mention a key figure without whose support the firm would never have seen dollar one from the U.S. government.

U.S. Representative Daniel J. Flood was a Shakespearean actor who appeared in more than fifty performances before cutting short his stage career for law school. After obtaining his degree, he rose to become a deputy attorney general in Pennsylvania before making his initial run for Congress in 1944. Born in Hazleton, Pennsylvania, and a graduate of Syracuse University, Flood's first term in Washington, D.C., ended in defeat in 1946. He was elected again in 1948 and stayed for two terms before losing again in 1952.

The loss stung Flood, and he promised it wouldn't

happen again. When he was elected again in 1954, Flood would remain in Washington for a quarter of a century, and his longevity was due, in large part, to the friendship he cultivated with Russell Bufalino.

Schooled by Stefano Magaddino during his early years in Buffalo, Bufalino was keenly aware of the profitable relationships and widespread protection that spawned from political power. Nurturing political and law enforcement contacts was a lesson reinforced by Frank Costello, and understanding the value of the right to vote was invaluable for anyone who had designs on growing a business.

Beginning in the 1940s, Bufalino's handpicked political candidates routinely won local and county elections, many of them often rigged with the votes of dead people while senior citizens were often rousted from their homes to vote for the preferred candidates.

Alliances with law enforcement and local, state and federal politicians were simply considered good business, and it didn't hurt if you could count among your friends a U.S. congressman or senator.

Daniel Flood was keenly aware of Bufalino's growing influence throughout the region. The garment industry especially had remained under Bufalino's thumb, and despite his fearsome reputation, politicians quietly courted Bufalino for his support. Flood was no exception. Following his defeat in 1952, Flood clearly saw the need to have a friend like Russell Bufalino, which set the stage for a long-standing association.

Upon returning to Washington, Flood cemented what

was a burgeoning reputation as a showman. He wore a waxed mustache that, combined with his sartorial expertise, gave him the audience he craved during his days as an actor. Known as "Dapper Dan," Flood's likability masked a serious side that saw him steer hundreds of millions in grants and contracts to his constituency in Luzerne County. Flood chaired the powerful Subcommittee on Labor, Health, Education and Welfare of the House Appropriations Committee, which put him in the very important and enviable position of overseeing the billions doled out each year to cities and states for development projects.

For Bufalino, that meant virtually having the keys to the taxpayer's bank.

Flood steered tens of millions in lucrative contracts to his home district, and among those benefitting from Flood's influence was Medico Industries, which gained millions in assignments for military equipment and armaments that U.S. forces would use in Vietnam against the North Vietnamese and Vietcong. Medico's offices had long served as a staging area for Bufalino and his crew. Bufalino maintained an office there, while several Bufalino family members claimed legitimate jobs at Medico, among them, James Osticco and associate Angelo Son, who actually held a degree in electrical engineering from Lehigh University.

Bufalino's alliance with Daniel Flood was but one example of Bufalino's political prowess. On the state and county level, Bufalino money flowed to an assortment of judges, county officials and local police chiefs, ensuring there would be few interruptions of his myriad of businesses, legitimate and illegitimate.

Among his legitimate businesses, Bufalino expanded into several esoteric areas such as television production. In 1965, he purchased the Washington, D.C., rights to the closed-circuit television broadcast of the Sonny Liston–Cassius Clay fight in Lewiston, Maine. It was a rematch of a bout the previous year, in which a young Clay stunned the heavyweight champion with a sixth-round technical knockout. The second bout, on May 25, 1965, was even shorter, with Liston hitting the canvas in the second round in a controversial ending in which some suggested that Liston took a dive.

Bufalino had, over the years, managed several fighters, including a local Dunmore fighter named Jerry Tomasetti, whom Bufalino took to New York to help get his boxing license. Bufalino's partner in the boxing business and the closed-circuit television venture was Al Flora, the former boxer from Baltimore who became his driver, bodyguard and business partner.

By the late 1960s, Bufalino's legitimate business interests included junkyards, garment factories and local hotels, including a Howard Johnson's, and he took a cut, usually 10 percent, from anyone who sought to set up a business within his geographical home base. Bufalino also had facilitated loans to several resort owners in the Poconos.

Now in his midsixties, Bufalino was still embroiled in his battle with the government over his deportation and was virtually out of gas and on his last appeal. His attorneys were costing him a small fortune, and Bufalino did everything he could to make sure he collected every dime owed to him. At the same time, he had several run-ins with the law. He was indicted in 1969 and accused with two others affiliated with Stefano Magaddino of plotting to transport more than fifty stolen television sets from Buffalo to Pittston. They were color sets and valued at $35,000. The charges, like most other cases against Bufalino, eventually evaporated.

Among his illegitimate interests, which still included gambling, extortion, loan sharking and prostitution, Bufalino counted labor racketeering as his bread and butter, and that included the money he made off the loans made from the Teamsters pension fund. So it was with great interest, and self-preservation, that he kept his good left eye closely on his friend Jimmy Hoffa.

AFTER FINALLY EXHAUSTING his appeals from his 1964 convictions, Jimmy Hoffa reported to the federal prison at Lewisburg, Pennsylvania, in 1967, and control of the Teamsters union was transferred to Hoffa's chief lieutenant, Frank Fitzsimmons. Unlike Hoffa, whose sheer will could force even the strongest of men to break and bend to his wishes, Fitzsimmons was a conciliator, a bear of a man who simply sought to make everyone happy.

Fitzsimmons was also far more politically astute than Hoffa, and with his mentor behind bars, Fitzsimmons began the process of decentralizing the Teamster organization. Instead of just one man, which had been Hoffa, calling the shots, Fitzsimmons put many of the union's major decisions in the hands of regional directors. And that included the Teamsters' business dealings with organized crime.

Hoffa had been in bed with the mob for thirty years and made himself directly available to the mob's hierarchy. Fitzsimmons sought to insulate himself and the upper Teamster echelon and laid down a new edict that any organized crime boss seeking favors or money could simply contact his local Teamster representative. Hoffa was furious with Fitzsimmons, but the new organizational setup was fine with the mob hierarchy, including Bufalino. Everyone knew Bufalino was a Hoffa man, but he was a businessman first, and it had quickly become clear that under Fitzsimmons, the financial floodgates would open, given the new, acting Teamster boss was quietly making inroads with President Richard M. Nixon.

The Teamsters had officially endorsed the Democratic ticket led by Hubert Humphrey in the 1968 presidential election. The earlier candidacy of Robert F. Kennedy had sent shivers throughout the underworld, but when the younger Kennedy met his violent demise in Los Angeles in June 1968, the underworld exhaled again.

Nixon wanted the Teamster support and had promised to eventually pardon Hoffa. Only the timing would have to be such where it would be Fitzsimmons, and not Hoffa, who remained in control. Under Fitzsimmons' new decentralization edict, hundreds of millions were being lent from the Teamster pension funds at an unprecedented scale, with a good portion of the money now supporting mob-controlled casinos in Las Vegas, which was fast becoming the new Havana. Fitzsimmons was also fueling cash to Nixon and his attorney general, John Mitchell. Following Nixon's election, underworld prosecutions nosedived, while many other FBI probes were simply dropped. The Justice Department under John Mitchell had other priorities, and the mob was allowed to flourish.

ON OCTOBER 7, 1971, the U.S. Court of Appeals denied Russell Bufalino's deportation appeal and ordered that he be immediately sent to Italy. The decision wasn't surprising and almost expected. Bufalino should have been booted from the country long ago, but he had managed to use one unorthodox delaying tactic after another. He had one last appeal, and if that didn't work, there was yet another option. In the meantime, his immediate attention was diverted to a book that drew the ire of many Mafiosi.

Published in 1969, *The Godfather* told the fictional story of Vito Corleone, a Sicilian immigrant who wielded great power while leading his criminal family in 1940s New York. Written by an Italian, Mario Puzo, the book was a bestseller that spent sixty-seven weeks on the *New York Times* book list, and Paramount Pictures was adapting the story into a film starring Hollywood legend Marlon Brando in the title role.

A younger segment of *La Cosa Nostra* took exception to what it expected would be yet another attempt to show Italians in a most unfavorable light. Joe Colombo, who headed New York's Colombo family, boldly formed the

Italian American Civil Rights League to combat what it perceived as Italian American discrimination by the FBI. During one of its first rallies, in New York in June 1970, more than 100,000 people were in attendance to show their support. The league subsequently grew, and chapters opened in different cities across the country, including Pittston, Pennsylvania.

When word surfaced that Paramount was adapting *The Godfather* to film, it was Colombo who sent word that his new organization would use its Teamsters contacts to stop the production, and another rally, this one at Madison Square Garden in New York, was held to protest the film. The producers also had to deal with Frank Sinatra, who was mocked in the book through the character of Johnny Fontaine, a womanizing singer whose ties to the Corleone family brought him fame and fortune and was seen as far too close to Sinatra's relationship with Chicago mob boss Sam Giancana. Sinatra did what he could do to stop the film.

Colombo later had a change of heart and signed off on the movie after reviewing the script and requesting, and receiving, the removal of the lone use in the film of the word *Mafia*. It seemed too simple a solution, and it was. Unbeknownst to but a few people, the peace came on orders of other high-ranking Mafiosi, specifically Russell Bufalino.

*The Godfather* wasn't so much a gangster movie as it was a film about a proud and successful immigrant American family. When Bufalino heard that the young director, Francis Ford Coppola, was turning Puzo's book into a

Shakespearean tragedy, he was intrigued. Every movie based on Italian Americans always showed dimwitted, half crazed and violent thugs terrorizing the public, the police and even their own families.

*The Godfather* was different and to a certain extent justified the very existence of organized crime as a group that, under Vito Corleone, provided the public with simple pleasures like gambling, alcohol and sex. Politicians were bought, as were police captains, but the Corleones were far more representative of corporate America than your run-of-the-mill mob family.

Bufalino's fascination with the film was odd, given that throughout his life he had no use for publicity of any kind. Few photos were taken of him, aside from FBI agents peering from some unseen location. But Bufalino's intellect absorbed the idea of a Sicilian immigrant who made his place in America despite the steepest of odds, and it was Bufalino who signed off on the mob's support of the film. Colombo was ordered to make peace with the production, which he did after extracting minimal commitments from the producers, several of which were never honored, including a promise to give the proceeds from the New York premiere to Colombo's group.

Bufalino's influence also led to several casting decisions. Singer Al Martino had coveted the role of Johnny Fontaine, but Coppola had no interest in giving it to him. Martino had a number-one single, "Here in My Heart," in 1952 and later played the casinos in Las Vegas, opening for acts including Dean Martin and Jerry Lewis. But he was among a second-tier group of singers who had been forced to leave the country in the 1950s after a spat with his managers, who were really mob guys who took over his contract. It was Angelo Bruno, the Philadelphia boss, who brokered his return in 1958, and Martino returned to the club circuit.

When casting began for *The Godfather*, Martino invited Coppola and other members of the production to Las Vegas, where he spent nearly $25,000 on a party filled with booze and pretty showgirls. Despite the elaborate and costly effort, Coppola had another singer, Vic Damone, penciled in for the role. Desperate, Martino turned to his real godfather, Russell Bufalino, who was the one person he knew who could successfully weigh in on the matter. Within a week, Damone curiously bowed out, and Martino got the coveted role.

Al Lettieri was also looking to be cast in the movie. The New York–born actor sought the role of Virgil "the Turk" Sollozzo, the violent drug dealer who plotted the assassination of Vito Corleone after the don declined to finance Sollozzo's heroin operation.

Lettieri's dark hair and complexion and menacing features gave him the look of a real wise guy. In fact, Lettieri *was* a real mobster, having worked for the Genovese family as an associate since he was a teen. Lettieri had worked in restaurants owned by his two "uncles," Tommy and Patsy Eboli, who were the caretakers of the Genovese family while its leader, Vito Genovese, sat out most of the 1960s serving an extended prison term that emanated from his arrest at Apalachin in 1957. Genovese died in prison in 1969, leaving control of his family to the Eboli brothers.

Lettieri ran numbers and did other odd jobs for his uncles before being entrusted with overseeing several Genovese-owned restaurants. After fleeing to England to escape some family-related trouble, Lettieri returned to New York and took up acting and eventually got his first role in a 1964 television movie, *The Hanged Man*, with Robert Culp and Vera Miles. It was Bufalino who quietly put the word out that Lettieri would make a perfect Sollozzo. During preproduction, Lettieri took some of the actors and crew, including Al Pacino, James Caan and Marlon Brando, to Patsy Eboli's home in Fort Lee, New Jersey. Patsy would later be on the set as an advisor.

Now carrying the mob's blessing, other real gangsters were cast in the film, including Lenny Montana, who secured the brief but legendary role of Luca Brasi. Montana was a huge man who got the part inadvertently after showing up on the set one day as a bodyguard to another, younger gangster during filming on Staten Island.

Bufalino visited the set, too. For years, Bufalino had little use for actors or singers, especially Frank Sinatra, who he thought was a wannabe-tough guy who only threatened to raise his fists with a belly full of booze and several bodyguards nearby to step in. But Bufalino bought into *The Godfather*, and he spent time with Marlon Brando inside his trailer in Lower Manhattan's Little Italy neighborhood complaining about his deportation case while giving him a few pointers on mob etiquette.

When *The Godfather* premiered, in 1972, it was a smash hit that later won Academy Awards for Best Picture and Best Actor for Brando, whose Oscar-winning performance was, for those who knew Russell Bufalino, a wonderful imitation of him.

On July 16, 1972, four months after the film premiered, Tommy Eboli was gunned down on a Brooklyn street, shot five times as he was nearing his car. Leaderless, a vacuum at the top of the Genovese family would yet again be temporarily filled by Bufalino, who took over the family while the Commission considered a permanent solution.

# TWELVE

In March 2007, Pennsylvania State Police deputy commissioner Ralph Periandi resigned, calling an end to a thirty-two-year career. The disappointment over the decision by the state Gaming Control Board to give a slots license to Louis DeNaples notwithstanding, Periandi's dealings with the Rendell administration opened his eyes to the kind of backroom political dealings he only heard whispers about.

Just a month earlier, state senator Vince Fumo was indicted on 137 counts, including mail fraud, wire fraud, obstruction of justice and conspiracy. Fumo allegedly used his position in the Senate to steal taxpayer money and use state workers for his own personal pursuits, including construction on an addition to his Philadelphia home. He also allegedly stole $1 million in state funds and steered $1 million from one of his charities into his own pocket.

The charges were the culmination of a lengthy FBI probe into political corruption, and Periandi could only think back to his meeting in Philadelphia two years earlier. He had guessed the FBI was zeroing on Fumo, but he had never gotten an answer, until now. The supposed task force had been decidedly one-sided as the feds had their priorities and the state police did all the legwork with its investigation. For Periandi, watching as DeNaples was guided through the wall of legitimacy was hard to take for a law-and-order man, and Periandi's enthusiasm for the job had waned. But there would be some satisfaction, and it would come from knowing that Dauphin County district attorney Ed Marsico would soon empanel an investigative grand jury to probe DeNaples, the gaming board and, hopefully, Ed Rendell and his administration.

The first subpoenas were issued in May 2007, and they directed the Gaming Control Board to provide all information it had relating to the licensing of Louis DeNaples. The board immediately contacted DeNaples and his attorneys to tell them about the investigation.

In July, the grand jury heard from several people, and among them was the prosecution's star witness, Billy D'Elia.

D'Elia's agreement with the federal government called for him to plead guilty to a conspiracy charge in return for his cooperation in other ongoing investigations, either on the federal or state level. During his interviews with Rich

Weinstock and Dave Swartz, he had drawn a road map of his lengthy involvement with DeNaples, and spoke at length about DeNaples' long relationship with Russell Bufalino.

D'Elia repeated his story before the grand jury, recounting a friendship with DeNaples that dated back to the 1960s, when he was getting his feet wet as an associate of the Bufalino family. D'Elia told the grand jury of the business deals they did together, his protection of De-Naples when confronted with problems posed by other mob families in New York and New Jersey and, of course, their long-standing personal relationship.

Some of D'Elia's more riveting testimony centered around DeNaples and Bufalino. DeNaples was so important to the family, said D'Elia, that Russell Bufalino approved the plan to fix DeNaples' 1977 fraud trial, which ended in a hung jury.

Clarence Fowler, aka Shamsud-din Ali, the Philadelphia Imam now serving a seven-year prison term for racketeering and defrauding the city of Philadelphia, testified about several meetings he had with DeNaples, one of which was captured on an FBI phone wiretap where they discussed, among other things, the removal of hazardous material from Philadelphia to one of DeNaples' landfills.

Another witness, Louis Coviello, had known DeNaples since childhood, babysitting for his daughter Lisa, and was friends with DeNaples' brother Eugene. Coviello's father, Louis Sr., was among the men prosecuted with DeNaples in the 1977 fraud probe. Coviello had been a star running back at Dunmore High School in the late

1960s and went to Texas A&M on a football scholarship. But he was homesick and returned home within a month, landing on the streets of Scranton and Dunmore doing odd jobs for his father and DeNaples.

In 1977, Coviello and another man were convicted of shooting a drug dealer. Coviello claimed his innocence, saying he was present but didn't pull the trigger and had no idea the other man even had a gun. Coviello was convicted and sentenced to life in prison despite assurances, he said, from DeNaples that he would be provided with the legal help and muscle to keep him out of jail.

Coviello had spent thirty years in prison, nearly half the time in solitary confinement for breaking one rule or another. He was now at the state prison at Frackville, which was just off I-81 about an hour northwest of Harrisburg. Of medium height, with the strength of a bull and hampered by a terrible stutter, Coviello had come to the attention of the FBI, U.S. Secret Service, the gaming board's Bureau of Investigations and Enforcement (BIE) and state police troopers Rich Weinstock and Dave Swartz around the same time.

The Secret Service and FBI visited with Coviello twice in 2007 to talk about a money-laundering probe involving DeNaples. BIE's interest came a year earlier during its background check as DeNaples sought a gaming license. Coviello was of such importance to BIE that during DeNaples' closed-door suitability hearings in December 2006, BIE had Coviello on the phone from prison to help them sort out DeNaples' vague responses. When confronted about particular details about his past, DeNaples became angry and displayed a side not even his attorneys wanted to see. And he had no idea BIE was getting its information in real time from Coviello.

Weinstock and Swartz also spent time with Coviello, having visited with him several times at the Frackville prison. Troubled since youth and cognizant of his terrible stutter, Coviello spoke slowly, detailing his long relationship with DeNaples and his family and his bitterness over how DeNaples abandoned him after his conviction.

It was clear that after all these years, Coviello's anger toward DeNaples was still raw.

"He told me and my father he would take care of this. That I wouldn't go to prison. He knew I didn't shoot anyone, but at the trial they said I was the one with the gun. They let me sink," Coviello told the troopers.

Then Coviello became reflective, and he told the troopers that his prison sentence could have been retribution from God for a murder he did commit years earlier. Coviello told how he had walked into Community Medical Center in Scranton and into the room of a man who was recuperating from a heart attack. The man was a witness in an upcoming trial of Bufalino associate Philip "Fibber" Forgione, and when Coviello walked into the room, he closed the door, took a pillow and placed it over his head, smothering him to death.

The papers said the man died of heart failure, and neither Coviello nor Forgione were ever implicated in the murder.

"God has a weird way of settling debts," said Coviello.

Before the troopers left the prison, Coviello pulled out

several letters he had written over the past year or so to the state gaming board and to Greg Matzel, the co-owner of Pocono Manor who lost his bid to DeNaples for a slots license.

"You can use these. You can see the gaming board knew what it was dealing with," Coviello said.

The troopers took the letters and read them with great interest.

*December 26, 2006*

*Dear Mr. Matzel,*

*I don't have time for chit chat so I'm going to be blunt. Do what you think is best.*

*I watched the hearings with interest. Since your lawyers wrote me on September 8th I have had 3 interviews with the Gaming Control Board and the State Police who work with the Gaming Control Board.*

*First off lets not pretend to fool each other. I knew you would have to send my letter to the Gaming Control Board. I did what I did for me and I used you and you used me. In here, a fair exchange is no robbery.*

*Listen to me, last Tuesday, the day before the hearings I was interviewed again and I was shocked to see that Louie still got the votes. Did you listen closely to Tad Decker's words of, those who receive licenses will still be investigated. I knew the first delay was due to me and I knew Tads words of caution are due to what's going on.*

*If you can appeal this decision appeal it. I was read parts of Louie's interview, he lied, he said he hardly knew me or my father.*

*In late 69 or 70 Louie had the Scranton Garbage Contract. There was a strike and SCAB workers were hired. My father was the Superintendent for Louie. My picture was in the Scranton Times under the title; Child Labor. I was like 13. How do you deny that. His brother was my best man at my wedding. Louie's whole family attended my wedding. My son and father in law either work for him now or did in the past. I slept in this guys house a whole summer when my parents were getting a divorce.*

*I drove his brothers corvette my senior year in high school.*

*Are these lies PERJURY?? Did you see his daughter Lisa, I use to baby sit for his kids.*

*The last words these cops told me was they'll be back.*

*You did not get a fair shake. I watched both your presentation and Louie's. I need you to push this. I'm not waiting for a reply either.*

*I have 2 more ACES to play. Send me an investigator if need be. Can you get a copy of his interview. You should have heard him blow up when incidents from the past were thrown at him.*

*You are the only one I don't suspect of taking a suit case full of money. I just had a visit today and the people who visited me were not contacted by the investigators and they told me last week they were seeing them on Thursday.*

You are not getting a fair shake and if you don't step up to the plate you won't get your bats.

Listen to this, Attorney Cognetti was the prosecutor who prosecuted Louie, my father and myself. He begged me to give Louie up and my chargers would be dropped, now he works for him. It doesn't take a rocket scientist to add this up.

I apologize for any typos but I am rushed for time tonight.

Good Luck,
Louis Coviello EA6952

———

April 11, 2007

Mr. Matzel,

Its 4 in the morning and if I don't get this out now it might not go for a few days. I know, you sent my last letter to the Gaming Control Board and they told me not to write you anymore. I guess if I followed rules I would have never spent 15 years in solitary confinement these past 29 years.

I'm sending this letter certified mail. Its a waste of money but I will know you received it. Did you know I sent Louie a certified letter just like this last summer. Yes sir, and he never told the Gaming Control Board about it. And I sent them a copy of the letter and the green card. Did you also know I have been interviewed

*7 times. I was interviewed the day before the hearings. As I was interviewed they were on the phone with a field agent as they showed me photos. I had a visit a few weeks ago and they verified past crimes. In fact they dug so far they showed me something I forgot about. This was a law suit that involved my father and Louis. This is the same Louie who for 84 pages denied hardly knowing me or my father. If you could get your hands on these 84 pages you could prove perjury. And its public information. Go to the courthouse, library and Scranton Times. The cops have it, they know.*

*So here's what I am thinking. The field agents are being over ruled by their superiors. That is, their being told to let it go. No doubt politicians are pushing to drop this.*

*I'm sure you were either watching the hearings or there when Louis presented his case. I'm sure you saw little Lisa. I use to baby sit for her. Her brother Doctor DeNaples just sent me a message that he wants to see me. He was my favorite. He never missed one of my games. His Uncle Eugene DeNaples is my son's God Father and my best man at my wedding. The cops know all this. I'm sure the church has records. February 5th of 1976. St. Anthony's church in Dunmore.*

*So tell me, how is it possible that Louie remembers seeing me around town. His exact words that were read to me where, "yeah, he was a kid from the neighborhood, he played football, he went to Texas A&M. I didn't really know him. And his father drove truck for me once in awhile. I think Louis is still in prison isn't he."*

*He didn't mention the certified letter I sent him nor the times in the past 29 years when I wrote him.*

*I hope you are getting the message. I read where you hired a lawyer in Pittsburgh. Your money would be better spent by sending me an investigator that could follow a map and give you concrete evidence. Then you could take this to the board and cry bloody murder.*

*I wasn't given the polygraph test and I know why. Then there would be more evidence that what I said is true. They told me, they knew I'm not lying so there is no need to give me one. In fact they told me when this process first started my credibility was like whale shit but its rising. The cops are amazed at my memory.*

*Louie knows I write you. I sent him a few letters since June. I told him to get my fucken money. Why didn't he report me. If someone tries to extort you wouldn't you call the cops? You wouldn't if you didn't want the information made public. And that's going to be my last resort. I'm going to tell you what to do. Before you send this to the Gaming Control Board. Go down the Scranton Times and Scranton Tribune Office and get a copy of every article on Louie. They have 6 folders of them. And in them articles is evidence that Louie lied when the board questioned him. Go back to 1968. Get the articles on the Scranton Garbage Strike. He had a contract with the city. My father was the Superintendent. Louie forgot about this.*

*I was in the paper as child labor when the strike was going on.*

*Excuse my typo. I need to know if you put me in your appeal. I don't care if you do, I just need to know.*

*Enclosed is a good book.*

*Respectfully,*
*Louis Coviello EA6952*

———

*May 2, 2007*

Mr. Matzel,

*I sent you a certified letter on April 11th. The postal service is tracing it now since I never received the green card back. I hope you received it. I have a rough draft of what I wrote. The gist of it is, you need to read the 84 pages that were read to me. It was an interview with Louie about my father and me. He lied many times and they know he committed perjury.*

*I sent a copy to the street and I will have it sent to you. I have been interviewed 7 times so far. They have tracked down people and verified past crimes.*

*I think the field agents are being over ruled by their superiors. Their being told to let it go.*

*If I can't get a certified letter to you then I'm not sure this will reach you. The bottom line is I told you in this certified letter how you can prove he perjured himself. Its public record. Get those transcripts of those closed door meetings.*

*Louie said he really didn't know me or my father.*

*My father and Louie where co-defendants in a law
suit in 1969, Louie's brother Eugene was my best
man and my son's Godfather. My father was also the
superintendent of the garbage workers when Louie had
the Scranton garbage contract in 1969. This was before
the Flood trial.*

*I read where you hired a lawyer in Pittsburgh. Your
money would be better spent by sending me an
investigator.*

*I was interviewed the day before the vote. I knew
what Tad Decker meant when he said, all law
enforcement agencies have been contacted. We both
knew the deck is stacked against you.*

*If you didn't receive a certified letter how will you
receive this. I'm tired of wasting my time. You think
their going to hand you a Gaming License when every
political figure that could be bribed was bribed.*

*Louie never reported the certified letters I sent him
and the Gaming Board had a copy of the letters and
green card.*

*Everybody knew Louie was getting the license except
you.*

*Louis Coviello EA6952*

TWO DAYS AFTER Billy D'Elia testified before the grand
jury in Harrisburg, Tad Decker announced at a press conference that he was resigning as chairman of the state
Gaming Control Board.

Decker had presided over the creation of what was envisioned as a multibillion dollar industry in Pennsylvania. He had steered the gaming initiative from its infancy to the licensing of nearly a dozen casinos. But now, amid a criminal probe of DeNaples and questions surrounding how he was awarded his license, Decker said it was time for him to step down. His new destination, he said, would be his old law firm Cozen O'Conner, the Philadelphia powerhouse that counted among its dozens of well-heeled clients one Louis DeNaples.

During his press conference in Harrisburg, Decker deflected any criticism of the DeNaples gaming license, saying the state police had signed off his application. His comments appeared in newspapers across the state the next morning, and among those who read the stories was Ralph Periandi.

Retired only five months, Periandi was stunned by Decker's comments. There was no way Periandi could allow those statements to stand without a response. So the next day Periandi was quoted in the *Allentown Morning Call* saying the gaming board had all it needed to deny the DeNaples license and that no matter what the police did, it was clear the DeNaples license was predetermined.

"My recommendation was to table this decision in granting a license. I couldn't tell the board the reason why, but we had a situation where we had an [investigation] that was running its course and we were not in a position to let anybody know. The gaming board had timelines, and we were taking second place to a licensing decision," Periandi said.

Periandi had been waiting two years to unleash his frustrations, and he zeroed in on Decker and the gaming board, saying, "It seems to me they weren't concerned about getting the fullest information possible on some of these people."

Decker's response in the same article was typical Decker bravado.

"A flat-out lie and figment of his imagination," said Decker of Periandi.

The state police, in an official statement, supported Periandi, saying the information concerning DeNaples was withheld from the gaming board, and the board knew it. Periandi's comments were followed by several other stunning revelations, including a report of an ongoing federal probe involving DeNaples and Ed Rendell centering on questionable contributions prior to gaining his slots license.

The *Morning Call* reported on a probe that centered on whether DeNaples had contributed $150,000 to Rendell just prior to gaining a slots license. In addition, several people closely associated with DeNaples gave more than $400,000 to Rendell. Among them was Thomas Karam, an energy executive with ties to DeNaples through a controversial company called Theta Land Corporation. Karam's business was natural gas, and the Wyoming Valley was part of the vast Marcellus Shale natural gas reserve, the largest reserve of natural gas in the country, which stretched from New York State through Pennsylvania into Ohio, Virginia and West Virginia.

Karam's prior contributions to Rendell never exceeded

$5,000, yet somehow he came up with $150,000, and investigators were probing whether the money was funneled from DeNaples to Rendell through Karam.

Before the grand jury would convene again, in late August, there was yet another stunning revelation. On August 22, 2007, the *Morning Call* reported that Thomas Marino, the U.S. attorney for the Middle District, which included Scranton and Harrisburg, had been recused from a federal probe of DeNaples because Department of Justice officials learned that Marino had given a personal reference to DeNaples for his slots application.

A few days later, the newspaper reported that Marino would resign. Even the most jaded followers of the De-Naples saga could not comprehend how a sitting U.S. attorney would, in good conscience, feel compelled to provide a recommendation for a convicted felon and a man with alleged ties to organized crime.

Marino's referral was discovered by members of his staff, who immediately reported Marino to Department of Justice officials in Washington, D.C. The DeNaples probe, which also included the Katrina trucks investigation, was transferred to the U.S. attorney in Binghamton, New York.

Marino, who was nominated by U.S. Senator Arlen Specter in 2002, denied he was resigning and would only say that DeNaples was an old friend and he would do the same thing again if asked. Six weeks later, Marino stepped down. He soon landed another job, hired by DeNaples for $250,000 a year as an in-house attorney for the Mount Airy Casino Resort.

Around the same time in Harrisburg, a Catholic priest was being led to the back door of the Dauphin County courthouse. The Rev. Joseph Sica had for the length of the gaming-application process provided an almost comical sight standing or sitting at DeNaples' side. Assigned by the Diocese of Scranton to serve as the chaplain of Mercy Hospital, Sica instead could be found with DeNaples during nearly every public appearance before the gaming board. Sica would be there supposedly as a spiritual advisor, but, to most observers, he was more of a "bodyguard," running interference for DeNaples and stepping between him and the media. It was the oddest of sights, a burly Catholic priest acting as a tough guy.

Sica spent the morning before the grand jury and was represented by attorney Sal Cognetti, who happened to be the former U.S. attorney who prosecuted DeNaples in 1977. Others who testified before the grand jury included James Decker, a former Lackawanna County official who was charged with DeNaples in the 1977 case; Sam Stratton Jr., an assistant business manager and the president of Laborers' Union Local 332 in Philadelphia; and Frank Pavlico, a Scranton-area man who was a close confidant of Billy D'Elia. Pavlico had been charged in the conspiracy case against D'Elia, who would later learn that it was Pavlico who agreed to wear a wire, which recorded D'Elia making a number of incriminating statements.

Although most grand juries operated in secret, Dauphin County authorities had witnesses assemble in a third-floor room that was easily accessible by reporters, who hovered in the hallways. In addition, the district attorney's website posted the dates when the grand jury would convene, alerting everyone, including the press. Reporters also had help identifying witnesses when Rich Weinstock called out their names to testify.

Unbeknownst to the media and others who had gathered on the third floor, several other witnesses, including former Philadelphia mayor John Street, were brought into the building via a back entrance and through the district attorney's office to a private entrance inside the grand jury room.

The grand jury would meet again in late September, after which the state Supreme Court once again stayed the case after DeNaples' attorneys had filed motions with the court seeking to quash the subpoenas and stop the probe.

The request was unusual, but the court ordered a halt pending its review. The court's order was fortuitous for DeNaples. His Mount Airy Casino Resort was scheduled to open in October, and had he been indicted, there was no telling if the gaming board would have allowed the facility to open its doors. Instead, thanks to the Supreme Court, the opening took place as planned. DeNaples, as expected, was greeted warmly. He said a few words, shook a few hands and then quickly left.

It took the court three months before denying the DeNaples motions and allowing the probe to continue. On December 27, 2007, the grand jury convened for a final time, and among those who testified was DeNaples' younger brother Eugene, who arrived with his attorney, J. Alan Johnson, of Pittsburgh, another former U.S. at-

torney from the Western District of Pennsylvania in Pittsburgh.

Three former U.S. attorneys had been hired or enlisted
on behalf of DeNaples or a family member to assist with
the gaming license or the grand jury. In addition to representing Eugene DeNaples, Johnson testified on behalf
of Louis DeNaples to debunk the 2001 federal affidavit
linking DeNaples to Billy D'Elia. Peter Vaira, a former
U.S. attorney in Philadelphia, was hired by DeNaples
to prepare his own background check for the gaming
board. And, of course, there was Thomas Marino, who
resigned after the Justice Department got word that Marino had provided a recommendation for DeNaples and
testified before the gaming board on his behalf.

Following his testimony, upon leaving the grand jury
room, Eugene made a wrong turn and walked out into
the elevator area, which was filled with reporters. He
quickly ducked into an elevator with Johnson, who said
the younger DeNaples had no comment.

Eugene DeNaples was the final witness. And now it
was up to the grand jury to decide his brother Louis' fate.

# THIRTEEN

Jimmy Hoffa's official release from prison was on December 23, 1971, just in time for Christmas.

He had spent nearly five years inside the Lewisburg prison, and by all accounts, he had been a model prisoner before his thirteen-year sentence was commuted by President Nixon on humanitarian grounds so he could care for his wife, who had suffered a heart attack.

Hoffa's release had actually been years in the making, but it came with a caveat: Hoffa couldn't "engage in the direct or indirect management of any labor organization" until March 1980. The terms weren't part of the original deal, and Hoffa only learned about it after he was released. He was furious and blamed a host of "rats" who turned on the one man who had brought the Teamsters to national prominence. The Teamsters was Hoffa's union, and in his mind, no one should or could run it while he was still alive.

The biggest rodent in Hoffa's eyes was Frank Fitzsimmons. Once a timid underling, Fitzsimmons grew strong during Hoffa's absence. The union had more members than ever, more revenues, and even more money in its pension funds. Most important, Fitzsimmons had a friend in the White House. His relationship with Nixon had flourished in just a few short years, and Fitzsimmons was now among one of the president's staunchest allies and supporters. Nixon had, during the 1971 Teamsters convention in Miami, made a surprise visit to support Fitzsimmons, who was seeking to officially replace Hoffa as Teamster president. With Nixon's help, Fitzsimmons won, and he repaid the favor during the 1972 election by throwing the great weight of the Teamsters union fully behind Nixon's reelection bid.

Hoffa fumed. With time deducted for good behavior, he most likely would have been out of prison by 1974 and eligible to seek the Teamsters presidency in 1976. He sent word to Bufalino that he would exact his revenge against Fitzsimmons while regaining control of the union. Bufalino told Hoffa to take the $1.7 million he had just converted from his Teamster pension and spend the rest of his days teaching and playing with his grandchildren, which is what Hoffa told the parole board he'd do to earn his way out to freedom.

Bufalino, like the rest of the mob bosses who sucked off the pension funds, didn't need Hoffa. His time had passed. The truth of the matter was that everyone was content under Fitzsimmons and his friend in the White House. There was new construction in Las Vegas, of which Bufalino and every major mob boss in the country now had interests, and the Teamster pension fund was now more like a child's piggy bank, where money could be withdrawn on a whim.

Bufalino knew his old friend was angry, but he firmly believed Hoffa would see the light and simply fade into the sunset. Bufalino had already pulled his cousin William from Hoffa's side several years earlier. The official story was that William Bufalino ended the relationship because he was tired of Hoffa's incessant complaining. But the breakup, in September 1967, came a month after Hoffa and Tony Provenzano came to blows inside the Lewisburg prison. Provenzano wanted his million-dollar-plus Teamster pension, which had been revoked following his felony conviction, and he sought Hoffa's help. Hoffa, after all, was still eligible to receive his pension despite his felony. But Provenzano's crimes reached a higher threshold, and Hoffa said there was nothing he could do. Provenzano was irate, and he turned to Bufalino for help, and he in turn recommended that Provenzano quiet down. Unbeknownst to Hoffa, the wheels were already spinning toward Fitzsimmons. The Hoffa situation was about to get ugly, but Bufalino had other pressing matters, and they focused on his pending deportation.

### IS THIS JUSTICE?

*It is our belief that sympathy and reconsideration should be accorded on the plight of Russell Bufalino*

*who is scheduled for deportation to Italy at the age
of 69.*

*He went to school here, registered for the draft, voted,
filed income tax and married an American girl. Bufalino has no criminal record except for a few traffic violations, no income tax evasion counts against him.
Bufalino did not burn draft headquarters or go around
as an anti-war pacifist. He did not cause violent damage
to this country as was done by many.*

*He had been under surveillance by the Federal Bu-
reau of Investigation for the years since the Apalachin
meeting. The F.B.I. is reputedly the greatest investigating bureau in the world. Yet, the only thing that Russell
Bufalino is being deported for is that they claimed he was
40 days old when he came to this country with his parents.*

*Russell Bufalino has helped many charitable organi-
zations and many people get into business. Hearsay statements connecting him to racketeering has not been listed
in any documentary form. Therefore we feel this action
against Mr. Bufalino is not justified.*

*Mr. Bufalino has an ordinary life span. The few years
he has left should be in the country he spent 69 years in.*

*The Italian American Civil Rights League*

The advertisement that ran in the local Scranton news-
papers was a desperate though feeble attempt to keep the
U.S. government from finally deporting Russell Bufalino.
His attorneys, led by Jack Wasserman, had argued his last

and final appeal on November 27, 1972, before the U.S. Court of Appeals, Third Circuit, in Philadelphia. Wasserman had managed to delay the case fourteen years, coming up with different motions such as arguing back in 1967 that his client was the victim of an "illegal wiretapping" by the FBI, and that the entire deportation proceeding should be stayed if not entirely dismissed. Wasserman also had argued that if Bufalino was sent to Italy, his life would be endangered.

The Board of Immigration Appeals had denied Bufalino's request on June 5, 1967, and again on October 7, 1971.

On January 30, 1973, the appeals court upheld the previous deportation rulings and ordered Bufalino to leave the country. The judges' opinion did not take kindly to the length of time it took to get to this point, and they delivered a scathing commentary on Bufalino's ability to tie up an immigration proceeding for so long.

"His present attorney has been in charge of the tactics, which have held petitioner in this country despite the fact that he deliberately and falsely asserted United States citizenship," said the judges.

Out of appeals, and out of time, Bufalino did what he had done several times before. He met with the other heads of the New York crime families and discussed the oversight and division of his businesses. Decisions were made on who would take over his interests in gambling, the Vegas casinos and the garment industry.

He had begun making preparations to fly to Italy when word came that the Italian government determined that

Bufalino was not a person of good character and not welcome in the country of his birth. Helping them with their decision was a suitcase filled with $1 million. The cost was high, but worth it. Italy's refusal meant Bufalino would stay in the United States.

Bufalino had been a major underworld figure since the 1940s, but now, at age seventy, he was never more powerful. He wasn't a member of the Commission and, to those who knew him best, being tagged as a supreme leader never captured his interest. He was content hiding under the camouflage of his Pennsylvania address knowing that no one, not even the FBI, would ever figure that someone who lived outside of Scranton could wield the kind of power and influence that he enjoyed.

Bufalino was in charge of his growing family in Pennsylvania, which now had more than fifty members. There were old, aging mainstays, such as capo James Osticco, who was arrested at Apalachin with Bufalino; Cappy Giumento, one of his closest confidants and sometimes driver; Joseph Scalleat, who ran the city of Hazleton; and Steven LaTorre, the lone remaining original member who was nearing ninety and in retirement, though still available for consultation when needed. Jack Parisi still lived in Hazleton. The former triggerman with Albert Anastasia's "Murder Incorporated," who had fled New York police and lived secretly in that city for years under the protection of Joseph Scalleat, was nearing seventy-five but remained a frightening presence. Only five feet six inches, Parisi began his work as a contract killer in the 1920s in Brooklyn, and since 1926, he had been arrested for a variety of crimes, including extortion, grand larceny, possession of a gun and murder. Following his move to Hazleton, Parisi joined Anastasia in several garment businesses, including the Nuremberg Dress Company and the Madison Dress Company, but he became a member of the Bufalino family and took up where he left off in New York, becoming Bufalino's most trusted triggerman long before some of those duties were transferred to Frank Sheeran, who also remained an important member of Bufalino's entourage.

There was also new blood led by William D'Elia, whom Bufalino had grown fond of and treated like a son. Bufalino had no children of his own, and the attentive D'Elia filled that void while serving as Bufalino's bodyguard.

In addition to his own family, Bufalino still maintained control over the Genovese family in New York, and he maintained a regular dialogue with the heads of New York's four other crime families.

Bufalino had, as he had for much of his life, avoided any major entanglements with law enforcement though he had one blip in 1974 when he was charged with fifteen other men with conspiring to extort two vending company officials in Binghamton, New York. Bufalino had a vending company, A&G Vending and Amusement, and he sought to erase the competition by bribing them out of business. On April 24, 1974, Bufalino was tried and acquitted of all charges. Three months later, in July 1974, his mentor, Stefano Magaddino, was felled by a heart attack at age eighty-two.

The old don, like Bufalino, was among the last of the Sicilian-born Mafiosi. For more than fifty years, Magaddino ruled over his upstate New York crime family and also maintained his place on the Commission. The faux pas over Apalachin nearly cost him his life. Another slipup, when police found nearly $500,000 in his son's home hidden in a suitcase in 1968, led to some discontent within his own family. Magaddino and a son, Peter, were already facing bookmaking charges when the money was found, and other family members believed Magaddino was holding out on them. The ensuing friction led to a split that was only resolved when Bufalino agreed to step in and take control over a portion of the family. With Magaddino dead, Bufalino moved quickly to consolidate the rest of his family in Buffalo and their interests elsewhere. By the end of 1974, Bufalino was now directly in charge of three crime families and personally controlled businesses in territories that stretched from New York City to Pennsylvania to upper New York State, Florida, parts of Ohio and Las Vegas.

At seventy years old, Russell Bufalino was at the pinnacle of his career and wielded incredible power.

But then came Hoffa, and *Time* magazine.

# FOURTEEN

---

Since his release from prison, in 1971, Jimmy Hoffa had become a growing irritant. He had played ball during his first year of freedom, supporting Richard Nixon and saying all the right things about the president's economic programs. Richard Nixon *was* good for the country, said Hoffa, and, more important, he was good for the Teamsters.

But Hoffa had a constant pain in his stomach, and it could only be cured by exacting his revenge against Frank Fitzsimmons and the other Teamsters, including Tony Provenzano, who Hoffa believed had betrayed him.

The secret condition attached to his pardon that prevented him from holding office until 1980 gnawed at him like a cancer, and after a year of public goodwill, Hoffa decided to fight the ban. He devised a strategy that would challenge the condition on constitutional grounds. How could the president of the United States insert such an onerous clause to a pardon when he didn't have the authority? Hoffa argued that the condition was not part of his criminal sentence, and it also could very well have violated his First Amendment right to freedom of speech.

Hoffa had told only a few of his staunchest supporters of his plan to retake the Teamsters, but more than a year after his release from prison, as word filtered about his plans, he made them public in April 1973 during a banquet in Washington, D.C. The news didn't necessarily surprise Fitzsimmons and the rest of the Teamster leadership, who heard about Jimmy's intentions from other Teamsters who earlier attended a testimonial dinner for Hoffa. It was Hoffa's sixtieth birthday, and the dinner was at the famed Latin Casino in Cherry Hill, New Jersey.

Russell Bufalino was there to celebrate with his old friend, but Fitzsimmons wasn't, having cited a previous commitment. The news of Hoffa's bid for a comeback was virtually ignored by the Nixon administration, which by now was consumed by the Watergate fiasco.

In February 1974, Hoffa began his public campaign to unseat Fitzsimmons, saying he was unfit to lead the Teamsters. During the months prior, Hoffa had obtained an affidavit from John Mitchell, who was now running Nixon's Committee to Reelect the President (CREEP), that stated that neither Mitchell nor anyone in the Justice Department "initiated or suggested the inclusion of restrictions in the Presidential commutation of James R. Hoffa."

The affidavit also said Nixon did not have any involvement in the restriction. The cost for the affidavit was a suitcase full of cash totaling nearly $300,000 that Hoffa gave to Frank Sheeran to personally deliver to Mitchell.

Sheeran had risen through the ranks to become an important member of the Teamsters since his first introduction to Hoffa years ago. From a Teamster boss in Delaware to a Teamster delegate, Sheeran had also continued his side work for Hoffa, mopping up his enemies. Sheeran was indebted to Hoffa and grateful for the opportunities that Hoffa provided, and he later visited Hoffa in prison but was disturbed to see how the solitary life affected his once proud boss. Hoffa tried to maintain a daily routine that included a regimen of push-ups along with his regular work duties. But prison life was monotonous, with much of your time spent locked in your cell. With each passing year, Sheeran could see Hoffa's slow, personal deterioration, and he knew his friend could never complete his sentence.

Sheeran would report back to his other good friend, Russell Bufalino, about Hoffa's progress. Bufalino never shared with Sheeran the reasons why Hoffa needed to remain behind bars. Fitzsimmons was a different and better fit compared to the autocratic Hoffa. He also didn't have a bull's-eye on his back that kept the attention of everyone, from the FBI to the media, glued to the Teamsters.

Hoffa would eventually get out, said Bufalino, but it would take a little time. Sheeran understood, and the conversation ended. There were never any long explanations from Bufalino. He was easy to read, even when he wasn't specific. When Bufalino wanted something done, he'd simply make a call, like the one he made to Sheeran during the summer of 1972.

It was late in the evening when Sheeran picked up the phone, and Bufalino told him to get "his little brother" for an errand. The little brother was a .32 revolver. Sheeran also brought along a "big brother," a .38. Sheeran wasn't told the target at first. It never worked like that. But the following day, he learned it was "Crazy" Joe Gallo.

Gallo was a New York–born gangster who had served eight years in prison during the 1960s on an extortion conviction and, following his release, became a bit of a celebrity. His outward personality endeared him to several actors, singers and film producers, and soon Gallo was spotted at local New York restaurants accompanied by one famous face after another. Gallo had supported Joe Colombo's Italian American Civil Rights League, but the men were rivals, and it was Gallo who was suspected of planning Colombo's shooting.

Colombo lingered in a coma for months after he was gunned down during one of his Civil Rights League rallies in New York. The shooting didn't sit well with certain members of the mob hierarchy, so when it was decided to dispose of Gallo, Bufalino handed the task to Sheeran, who simply walked into Umberto's Restaurant in Little Italy, stood by the bar for a few minutes and then turned and shot Gallo, who had been celebrating his forty-third birthday with his wife and friends. Seriously wounded, a bloodied Gallo picked himself up amid the screaming and confusion and ran toward the front door. Sheeran coldly shot him two more times before Gallo slumped outside on the street corner. Witnesses initially identified two shooters, which was fine with Sheeran.

Hoffa filed his lawsuit in March 1974, alleging he knew nothing about the restrictions on his pardon and, had he known, he would never had agreed to them. Hoffa also argued that since the conditions didn't come from the president or the attorney general, they were invalid since no one else could legally impose such sanctions. In July 1974, a federal judge in Washington, D.C., ruled against Hoffa, saying that since President Nixon signed the order, it was valid.

Hoffa appealed. A month later, Nixon resigned the presidency.

IN THE FALL of 1974, Jimmy Hoffa let it be known that he was going to exact his revenge against Frank Fitzsimmons by calling in pension loans after he won the Teamsters presidency in 1976.

The loans Hoffa was talking about were for casino construction projects in Las Vegas, projects in which members of certain families had majority interests. There were records, said Hoffa, and he was ready to turn them over to the proper authorities. Hoffa's talk made people nervous, though friends like Sheeran knew it was more bluster on Hoffa's part, and he made a point of telling that to Bufalino, who by now was growing concerned.

Bufalino asked Sheeran to set up a meeting with Hoffa at a Philadelphia bar and restaurant called Broadway Eddie's. When Hoffa arrived with Sheeran they were taken to the back, where Bufalino and Philadelphia boss Angelo Bruno were waiting for them. They dined over pasta, but during the meal, Bufalino raised the issue of Hoffa's run for the Teamsters presidency and suggested that Hoffa didn't have to run.

Hoffa's response was simple: he wanted to oust Frank Fitzsimmons.

Bufalino's way was to make his point, hear a response and then move on to another subject. Before turning to Bruno to signal the conversation was over, Bufalino stopped eating and looked Hoffa in the eyes before making his point, *a second time.*

"It would be best for everyone concerned if you reconsidered your position," said Bufalino.

Hoffa wasn't going to listen to reason, and before the men said their good-byes, Bufalino pulled Sheeran aside and told him to make Hoffa understand that he had no choice in the matter.

The following night, Bufalino and Hoffa joined a few thousand other friends at the Latin Casino in New Jersey for "Frank Sheeran Appreciation Night." Philadelphia mayor Frank Rizzo was there, and the pretty Golddigger dancers and Jerry Vale provided the entertainment. Sheeran sat at the dais with his wife and four children, while Bufalino had a front table next to the dais. Sitting with him were his wife, Carrie; his underboss, James Osticco; and Angelo Bruno.

Hoffa was the keynote speaker, and he spoke about how loyal Sheeran had been to him and to the Teamsters all these years. But the conversation from the night before still resonated, and Sheeran feared for his friend. Sheeran tried having a word with Hoffa, but the conversation was short and brief. Sheeran later told Bufalino there wasn't much anyone could do to change his mind and stop Hoffa from running.

There were some people, such as Tony Provenzano, who wanted to end Hoffa's life immediately, and with prejudice. Provenzano had enough of Hoffa's threats and believed the best way to deal with him was to silence him permanently. Bufalino, on the other hand, didn't share Provenzano's thoughts on the subject. Bufalino had known Hoffa for thirty years, and deep down he knew that Hoffa wasn't a rat. Even when word filtered at the Teamster convention in April 1975 that Hoffa was cooperating with the FBI, Bufalino didn't believe it, and his faith in Hoffa was restored when Hoffa took the Fifth Amendment during testimony before a grand jury investigating his old Detroit local in May 1975. But others weren't so sure, and the groundswell within the ranks of organized crime for Hoffa's untimely end grew stronger. Bufalino kept them at bay, and Hoffa remained alive longer than others had wanted.

# FIFTEEN

The U.S. Senate Select Committee to Study Governmental Operations with Respect to Intelligence Activities was formed in January 1975 to gather information on the CIA and FBI. The Senate wanted to take a closer look at the nation's intelligence operations after a series of articles that appeared in the *New York Times* in late 1974 revealed that the CIA was involved in toppling foreign governments and spying on U.S. citizens.

The committee, headed by U.S. senator Frank Church, R-Idaho, began holding hearings to confirm whether the CIA had conducted such operations, covert or otherwise, abroad and in the United States.

Following the end of World War II, the nation's attention was focused on its new Cold War with the Soviet Union, and stemming the tide of Communism was considered the number-one priority for the new agency.

Foreign leaders were secretly disposed, and governments were compromised while an ambivalent nation enjoyed its postwar prosperity.

The Church Committee looked at a variety of topics, including the CIA's plots to kill foreign leaders, among them the assassination attempts against Fidel Castro of Cuba. Surprisingly, the CIA confirmed that it not only tried to kill Castro, but in a shocking admission, the agency admitted that it had recruited members of the Teamsters and organized crime to help in that effort. The committee immediately sought to talk to Sam Giancana, Jimmy Hoffa and Johnny Roselli.

Word that the committee was looking at the mob's role in the CIA plots became public in the spring of 1975. But then, on June 9, 1975, came the *Time* magazine article. The piece was entitled, "CIA: Mafia Spies in Cuba," and it rehashed a previous article quoting "reliable sources" that claimed the CIA had recruited Giancana and Roselli to assassinate Fidel Castro. But the new story went a step further, and identified Russell Bufalino and two associates, James Plumeri and Salvatore Granello, as having worked with the CIA to help with the preparation of the Bay of Pigs invasion. According to the story, the CIA learned that Bufalino, Plumeri and Granello had left $450,000 in Cuba before fleeing the island (it was closer to $1 million), and the agency decided to recruit the men to conduct surveillance with their Cuban sources to gauge the potential success of an invasion and to help identify roads leading into Havana. The gangsters supposedly gave little, if any, information.

Bufalino had never before been implicated in the CIA plots, which were first mentioned by journalist Jack Anderson in 1970. After Anderson's column appeared, people began to die. Granello was found dead first, in an upstate New York cornfield, shot several times in the head. Plumeri, a longtime Bufalino associate, had been strangled in his car a year later.

The matter seemed to fade away, until the Church Committee decided to take a closer look. On June 19, ten days after the *Time* piece was published, Giancana was entertaining a small group of friends and family at his modest brick home in suburban Oak Park, Illinois. He had just returned from Houston, where he underwent a successful gallbladder operation, and the small affair was a sort of welcome-back-home dinner.

Giancana, sixty-six, had given up his top role in the Chicago mob years earlier. After a lengthy stay in Mexico, he was subpoenaed to testify before a grand jury that was probing organized crime activity in Chicago. Giancana testified once and gave prosecutors nothing.

After his party broke up and his guests left, just before midnight, Giancana walked down to his basement kitchen to fry some sausages and spinach. Someone was with Giancana, someone he knew and trusted, because soon after starting his meal, he was taken down by six gunshots to the mouth and neck with a .22 pistol.

Police initially believed Giancana got what he had coming. It was, by all accounts, a standard mob rubout, save the use of a .22 handgun, which was somewhat unusual. Another theory soon made the rounds, and that was that Giancana was done in by the CIA. He was scheduled to testify before the Church Committee, and some thought that Giancana might actually discuss his role in the agency's attempts to kill Fidel Castro. The aging Roselli, now sixty-nine, had testified a few days earlier before the committee and apparently made such a good showing that the committee wanted to hear more.

But CIA Director William Colby quickly doused any notion the CIA had a role in Giancana's murder.

"We had nothing to do with it," he said.

With no leads and few clues, the case quickly grew stagnant.

With Giancana gone, plans were being made in Scranton to address Jimmy Hoffa. For more than a year, Russell Bufalino had fought and lobbied to keep Hoffa alive amid his loud boasts and threats to turn over sensitive information on Teamsters loans and to bare all about the union's ties to the mob. The threats were more like a defense mechanism for Hoffa against the calls by the Teamster hierarchy and Mafiosi to step aside. Hoffa didn't just want the Teamsters back; he wanted his revenge against those who stripped him of his title and forced him to part ways with an organization he had helped build while spilling his own blood.

Hoffa no doubt held many secrets from the past. Secrets about the Kennedy assassination, Cuba, the fleecing of the Teamster pension fund and much more. And word filtering through underworld circles was that he threatened to use that information if anyone tried to stop him from regaining his union.

For his part, Bufalino kept reassuring others, including Santo Trafficante and Carlos Marcello, that Hoffa was simply boasting. But Bufalino's tone quickly changed after he was named in the *Time* article, and he once again called on his old friend Frank Sheeran.

THE WEDDING OF William Bufalino's daughter was scheduled to take place on Friday, August 1, 1975, at William's home in Grosse Pointe, Michigan, and among the more than 500 guests would be William's cousin Russell, Frank Sheeran and their wives.

Sheeran had tried throughout the summer to convince Hoffa to quiet down. Sheeran knew that the only reason Hoffa was still breathing was because of his friendship with Russell Bufalino. About a week before the wedding, Sheeran asked Bufalino for permission to call Hoffa at his cottage in Michigan. Sheeran desperately wanted again to try to talk sense into his friend, and Hoffa agreed to meet with him and Bufalino later that week when they were scheduled to arrive in Detroit.

The plan was for Sheeran and his wife to drive to Kingston, Pennsylvania, to have dinner with Russell and Carrie, and then they'd leave early Tuesday morning in Sheeran's Cadillac for the twelve-hour drive to Detroit. During dinner, Sheeran mentioned softly to Russell that he was going to be with Hoffa on Wednesday for his planned meeting with Provenzano and Tony Giacalone. A sizable portion of Hoffa's angst came from his continuing feud with Provenzano, and Hoffa believed if he could make peace with Tony Pro, then the rest was easy. But he wanted Sheeran there, just in case.

Bufalino said nothing and continued to eat. Not long after, the waiter told Bufalino he had a phone call. When he returned, Bufalino tugged on Sheeran's arm and whispered there would be a change of plans. Instead of leaving early the next morning, they would wait until Wednesday.

Sheeran didn't make any facial movements or ask any questions. He knew better. When Russell Bufalino said something, consider it an order. Sheeran said nothing to Hoffa. On Wednesday, Sheeran, Bufalino and their wives struck out early for the drive to Detroit. They were near Lake Erie when Bufalino suggested the women take a long smoking break. After they got out of the car, Bufalino and Sheeran drove to a small private airport, where a plane was ready to take Sheeran to Detroit.

# SIXTEEN

It was 10 P.M. on Wednesday, July 30, when Josephine Hoffa realized something was wrong.

Her husband had not returned home from his afternoon meeting at the Machus Red Fox Restaurant in nearby Bloomfield Township, which was less than twenty miles northwest of Detroit. Jimmy would usually call just to let his wife know he was all right, but the call never came, and by 8 A.M. the next morning, it was the police who were called, and thus began an investigation that ultimately resulted in more than two hundred FBI agents scouring for clues into the disappearance of Jimmy Hoffa.

Agents knew he had been at the restaurant, where they found his green 1974 Pontiac Grand DeVille. And they also learned that he went there intending to meet Tony Provenzano and Tony Giacalone, a high-ranking Detroit underworld figure. The two men denied they had scheduled a meeting, with each saying they were busy doing other things. Provenzano said he was getting a massage in New Jersey, while Giacalone was attending to one of his businesses.

A grand jury was impanelled in December 1975, and witnesses were subpoenaed, which aside from Provenzano and Giacalone consisted of a core group of men that included Charles O'Brien, a self-described "foster son" of Hoffa; Salvatore "Sally Bugs" Briguglio, a Detroit Teamster business agent; Thomas Andretta and his brother Stephen; Frank Sheeran; and Russell Bufalino. When they arrived to testify, they were accompanied by their attorney, William Bufalino, who advised each man to take the Fifth Amendment, which they did. Their testimony notwithstanding, the FBI was still able to put together a list of the chief suspects, and Bufalino, Sheeran and Provenzano were at the top.

The FBI developed a theory that Hoffa's boasting finally resulted in his demise, and the agency was sure he had gotten into a car with O'Brien and several other men, including Briguglio, around 2:30 P.M. that Wednesday afternoon.

Whatever happened after that was well planned and handled in a precision-like manner.

Along with the almost unbearable pressure exerted by the FBI, New York authorities had begun pressing Bufalino on his remaining garment-industry interests. Bufalino once controlled dozens of shops and manufacturing plants but now only had interests in six, including Fair Frox Inc., on New York's Fifth Avenue. Bufalino claimed he had been employed at Fair Frox since 1972 and collected a regular paycheck. The firm had been in business since 1956. In June 1976, Bufalino was interviewed by New York investigators at the Consulate Hotel. With him were Max Stein, Fairfrox's treasurer, and Al Flora, the ex-fighter who was now Bufalino's part-time bodyguard and chauffeur. The quizzing by the New York investigators was pointless but part of what Bufalino perceived to be the FBI's unrelenting effort to get him, or someone else involved in the Hoffa disappearance, to crack.

Two months later, in August 1976, Johnny Roselli met his demise. He was found dead, stuffed inside a drum floating in a Miami bay. Roselli had been tortured; no doubt his killers wanted to know exactly what he told the Church Committee.

Roselli had testified twice and gave the committee limited information. He was subpoenaed for a third time and scheduled to testify again in September, but his death, along with those of Giancana and, they believed, Hoffa, led the committee to deliver its incomplete report on the CIA's relationship with organized crime.

Despite its full-court press, the FBI couldn't develop enough evidence to charge anyone in the Hoffa case. But that didn't stop the agency from pursuing the chief suspects for other crimes. The government lived by a certain credo. If it couldn't prosecute you for one serious crime, it would surely get you on something else. And that was never more true than for the men who were the chief suspects in the Hoffa case, who were hounded for several years.

Union leader and Genovese family captain Tony Provenzano was subsequently tried and convicted in 1978 for the 1961 murder of a Teamster official. Anthony Giacalone was sentenced to ten years in prison for income tax fraud. Salvatore Briguglio, who had been under intense federal pressure and was connected with Provenzano to the 1961 Teamster murder, was shot and killed in New York in March 1978. Frank Sheeran was indicted in 1980 on several charges, including two murders, but he was acquitted. He eventually went to prison in 1982, following his 1981 conviction on labor racketeering, and was sentenced to thirty-two years in prison. Prosecutors had tried for several years to convince Sheeran to flip, even offering him a limited prison term if he would tell all he knew about the Hoffa murder and Russell Bufalino. Sheeran declined.

As for Bufalino, the slightest of threats from a man who spent a lifetime saying little gave the FBI all it needed to put the Quiet Don away for life.

ON THE MORNING of October 27, 1976, FBI agents from Philadelphia arrived at Russell Bufalino's home in Kingston to take him into custody on federal extortion charges related to a run-in Bufalino had with a Brooklyn bartender, Jack Napoli, who had used Bufalino's name as an introduction to a jewelry dealer who had diamonds Napoli had wanted. A federal grand jury in New York handed down the indictment against Bufalino and three other men. When the agents awakened Bufalino, now seventy-two, they allowed him to dress before taking him to a preliminary hearing in Wilkes-Barre, where he was released on $50,000 bond.

Around the same time in Brooklyn, FBI agents knocked on the door of the Bensonhurst home of Joseph Lapadura, seventy-two, who was one of the other men included in the indictment. Lapadura, a talkative fellow, had for years run floating crap games for Bufalino and had numerous arrests dating back to 1922. He told the agents he didn't know why he was being arrested but said he was willing to talk about his old friend. The two men had been friends for years, often meeting at the Vesuvio restaurant, and as far as Lapadura knew, Bufalino's only business was a dress manufacturing company in Manhattan. Lapadura was arraigned and released on $10,000 bond.

According to the indictment, Napoli bought the diamonds for $25,000, but the check he wrote bounced. When word got back to Bufalino that some low-level wise guy not only bounced a check buying stolen diamonds, but had used Bufalino's name in the process, the old don was furious.

Napoli got wind that Bufalino was unhappy, and he ran to the FBI. Napoli was subsequently called to a meeting at the Vesuvio restaurant, and when Napoli arrived, Bufalino couldn't control himself. Napoli was a large man at six feet six inches and around 240 pounds, yet Bufalino threatened to kill him with his own hands unless he returned the diamonds immediately.

"I'm going to kill you, cocksucker, and I'm going to do it myself and I'm going to jail just for you."

It was the rarest of exceptions to see Bufalino that angry, but what Napoli did was, in Bufalino's mind, beyond disrespect. Napoli had taken Bufalino's name and stomped on it. Napoli was told to make good on the diamonds. Unbeknownst to Bufalino, Napoli already knew he was in trouble and ran to the FBI. Napoli had been wired for the meeting, and everything Bufalino said was caught on tape.

Following his indictment, Bufalino's solution to beat the rap was to kill Napoli before he could testify. For help, Bufalino reached out to Jimmy "the Weasel" Fratianno.

Aladena James Fratianno was born in 1913 in Naples, Italy, and his family later immigrated to Cleveland, Ohio. As a teenager, Fratianno committed a variety of petty thefts and earned the nickname Jimmy the Weasel after throwing a rotten tomato at a policeman and running away. The act caught the attention of some older boys, who said, "Look at him running, just like a weasel." The cop wrote on his report, "They called him a weasel," and the name stuck.

In 1946, Fratianno moved to Los Angeles, where he owned several businesses, including a cigar store in Santa Monica, that were fronts for bookmaking, loan sharking and other illegal activities. He became a made member of the Los Angeles mob in 1946 and over the next thirty years took part in ten murders. In 1960, an argument with the mob hierarchy forced Fratianno to seek protection in Chicago under Sam Giancana. He was sent back to Los Angeles in 1975 to help run that family following internal discord.

In 1977, Fratianno became a government witness after he was charged with the murder of Danny Green, a union official in Cleveland who was killed after someone put a bomb under his car. It was Fratianno who introduced Green's killer to the Cleveland mob. Promised no more than five years in prison for his various crimes if he cooperated, Fratianno served only twenty-one months and was placed in the Witness Protection Program. Fratianno told the feds about Bufalino's plot to kill Jack Napoli. Fratianno said he first met Bufalino in September 1976 at the Rainbow Room in New York. Gangsters from around the country had all come to New York to see Frank Sinatra, who was making his second appearance at the Westchester Premier Theater, in nearby Tarrytown. The 3,500-seat facility had opened a year earlier and was owned by three men, New York mobsters Gregory DePalma and Richard Fusco, and Eliot Weisman, a securities salesman, with the financial help of Carlo Gambino, who headed the New York family that now bore his name.

The Gambino money came with a steep 10 percent interest rate, but it didn't matter because the trio, who opened the venue with a Diana Ross concert in 1975, skimmed hundreds of thousands of dollars off the top from tickets, merchandise, food and parking. Sinatra had performed in April 1976 and returned in September 1976 to sold-out audiences. Unbeknownst to all, the theater and its owners were under federal investigation, led by a young assistant U.S. attorney, Nathanial Akerman.

Following Sinatra's September 1976 performance, Fratianno and several friends, including Mike Rizzitello, arrived at the Rainbow Room in midtown Manhattan. There, Fratianno first met Bufalino, who was introduced as the head of the Pittston family. Fratianno in turn was introduced as the acting boss of the Los Angeles family.

Bufalino pulled Fratianno over to the side, and the two men spoke for twenty minutes or so, then said good-bye. On his drive back to Westchester, Rizzitello told Fratianno that Bufalino relayed how a grand jury was investigating his role in an extortion plot and that he wanted someone who was planning to testify against him at the upcoming trial clipped. The "someone" was Jack Napoli, who had been in hiding with the help of the FBI. Bufalino had incredible contacts within the federal government and learned Napoli was running a pork store in Walnut Creek, California, which was near Fratianno's home in San Francisco.

Napoli was indeed in Walnut Creek. After he turned himself in to the FBI, he was taken to Washington, D.C., where he met with U.S. Marshall James B. Colosanto of the Witness Security Division. They in turn placed Napoli and his wife in Walnut Creek, which was about as far away as you could get from northeastern Pennsylvania. Napoli did open a pork store, as Bufalino had learned, but he fled the area owing $3,000 to Wells Fargo Bank, and no one knew where he was.

Two days later, a meeting was scheduled at Vesuvio and Fratianno, Rizzitello and Bufalino sat down to talk about Bufalino's problem. Fratianno agreed to help, and when he flew home, he spent some time in Walnut Creek trying to locate Napoli, but to no avail.

Six months later, in May 1977, Fratianno returned to New York for the third Sinatra concert at the Westchester Premier Theater, after which he drove into Manhattan to meet with Bufalino again at the Vesuvio restaurant.

Accompanied again by Rizzitello, Fratianno didn't have much to report.

"I looked for Napoli, but I couldn't find him," he said.

"Well, the guy might have left. I'll find some other way," said Bufalino, who remained free on bail.

Fratianno was later arrested on multiple charges, including the murder of Danny Green, and he made his deal with the FBI to become an informant.

Fratianno later testified against Bufalino, and it was enough for the charges to stick. Bufalino was found guilty on October 21, 1977, and sentenced to four years in prison.

Following his sentencing, the FBI bureau in New York sent a telex to then director Clarence M. Kelley trumpeting Bufalino's conviction.

*Russell Bufalino is the boss of his own organized crime family and controls the northeastern Pennsylvania region, as well as New York's southern tier. In addition to this, Bufalino spends approximately half of his time in New York City.*

*Bufalino is particularly well-known in the business community in the Wilkes-Barre–Scranton area of Pennsylvania, as well as by judges and local legislators in that area. Information from sources in Philadelphia indicated that the business community was following very closely the trial and conviction of Bufalino, as well as what type of sentence he would receive. It was their feeling that if Bufalino was not given time in jail on his conviction, then they would know that Bufalino had the Federal Government in his pocket and they would lose all respect for the criminal justice system.*

*Since Bufalino was sentenced, their faith in the criminal justice system has been rejuvenated and they now believe that a big mob figure can be brought to justice.*

*Bufalino's annual Italian American Civil Rights League Festival held in Wilkes-Barre was the subject of many cancellations from local public figures who had previously been guest speakers at this annual gathering.*

*The trial, conviction and sentencing was the subject of widespread newspaper and radio coverage in northeastern, Pennsylvania, Albany, Buffalo, and New York City, and had a very favorable effect on the communities in those areas.*

Bufalino remained free while he appealed his decision, which was denied, and on August 10, 1978, he reported to the Metropolitan Correctional Center in Manhattan, where he remained for six weeks. Federal judge Morris Lasker had approved an unusual furlough for Bufalino to attend his fiftieth wedding anniversary in September, and Bufalino was to remain in New York until after his furlough. When he arrived back in Pennsylvania for his brief visit, Bufalino was honored at a private party at a Howard Johnson's motel he owned, and Mafiosi from throughout the region, including New York, Philadelphia, Buffalo,

Pittsburgh and elsewhere, were in attendance. The men drank, discussed business and then said their good-byes. Bufalino would remain in charge, dictating orders from behind the prison walls to Edward Sciandra, James Osticco and Billy D'Elia.

Upon his return to New York, he was then sent to the federal prison in Springfield, Missouri, and then transferred to the Federal Institution at Danbury, Connecticut, which was a two-hour drive across I-84 from Scranton.

A medium-security facility, the prison houses many of its inmates in a dormitory-style setting, where beds are lined up next to each other in rows, and prison life is fairly simple. There's the morning wakeup, then breakfast before reporting to whatever job was assigned to you, then free time, dinner, some television, then lights out. It's during the free period where inmates can congregate by playing basketball or sitting around playing chess or even pinochle. From the day he was brought to the Danbury prison, Bufalino always showed a preference for pinochle. But aside from his card games, Bufalino spent a lot of his free time overseeing his vast family business. Unbeknownst to Bufalino, the FBI was ramping up a special investigation that would entail the "full-time surveillance of members of the Russell A. Bufalino Family."

Dubbed RABFAM, the investigation was headed by the FBI's Philadelphia office, and the focus of the probe was the Bufalino family's growing influence, particularly in labor racketeering, political corruption and infiltration of legitimate businesses. The Justice Department finally recognized Russell Bufalino to be a powerhouse within organized crime circles, as information received from several informants along with residual reports from the Hoffa investigation revealed Bufalino's immense power.

Among those targeted were Bufalino, Casper "Cappy" Giumento, Frank Sheeran and Billy D'Elia, and over the course of the next few years, the investigation would eventually require the assistance of more than a dozen bureaus throughout the United States, from Miami to Las Vegas.

IN 1979, THE Danbury federal prison accepted a new inmate, a motorcycle gang member named Stephen Fox. An eighth-grade dropout, Fox was once a member of the Gypsy Jokers motorcycle gang, after which he switched allegiances and joined the Pagans, a group of thundering nomads who earned their keep through drug trafficking, selling stolen property and murder. Fox had several previous arrests, including interstate transportation of stolen property in 1969 and 1970. Sentenced to ten years in prison, he served only two, but a parole violation in 1972 earned him a trip back behind bars. He was released to a halfway house in 1975 but escaped, pled guilty and was sentenced to another five years in prison. Prior to his capture, Fox rented several cars but failed to pay for them and also used a stolen credit card.

Sent to another halfway house in 1978, Fox escaped but was recaptured shortly after in Albany, New York, and immediately sent to the Danbury prison in July 1979, and placed in a bunk just across the row from Bufalino.

Now serving the second year of his four-year sentence, Bufalino befriended Fox, and the two men spent several hours each day playing pinochle and talking about trucks and mechanics and Fox's plans once he was released. At night they watched television together with several other inmates, including Gregory DePalma, the former co-owner of the Westchester Premier Theater doing a term for racketeering. During one evening-news program, Bufalino jolted forward when he recognized the face of James Fratianno.

"He's a rat and needs to be shut up," said Bufalino.

Fox was scheduled to be released in July 1980 to a halfway house again, but he needed a job or else he'd remain in prison. Bufalino said he knew a guy that ran a trucking company in New Jersey who would put him to work. Fox called the guy and was told he'd have a job waiting for him once he was released.

When Fox told Bufalino the good news, he replied, "See, I'm glad I could do something to help you get out of here. Just remember there may come a time when I may need you for something."

A week later, Bufalino pulled Fox aside and told him that once he was released he wanted Fox to fly out to California and take care of a matter involving a witness. His name, said Bufalino, was Jack Napoli, and he had tried to have the matter handled before, but it failed. Fox was told that upon his release he would report to his new job, where a package would be waiting for him with information regarding Napoli, his photograph and his location.

"He's in Walnut Creek, California, and I'm asking you do me this favor because no one will figure a connection. It will look like something to do with drugs. Just be careful, but remember if there is a slip up, it's on your shoulders, understood?"

Fox was released on July 18, 1980, and went to work for a company called Howard's Express. He also got $300 and a new car, thanks to Gregory DePalma, who told Fox to go to an Oldsmobile dealer in the Bronx, where waiting for him was a new Cadillac.

But Fox never made it to California. Shortly after his release, he bolted for Florida after learning that several loan sharks were looking for him. Fox had borrowed money before his latest prison stint and never paid it back, and the loan sharks wanted their money, or his head. Arrested again for violating his parole, Fox had some information he thought the government would want to hear, so he cut a deal.

The federal indictment against Russell Bufalino was handed down on December 30, 1980. When he walked out of the prison in May 1981, the indictment had been unsealed, and he was taken into custody by federal marshals and charged with conspiring to murder Jack Napoli. He was released on bail and kept under twenty-four-hour surveillance by FBI agents working on the RABFAM investigation.

Day after day since 1978, FBI agents had reported diligently on the activities of the Bufalino family. In a telex sent from the Philadelphia bureau to FBI headquarters in Washington, D.C., on August 15, 1980, agents noted the extensive criminal activities, including loan sharking, bank fraud, jury tampering, obstruction of justice, interstate transportation of stolen property (jewelry, furs, etc.) and corruption of public officials. The telex also noted that in October 1979, the Italian American Civil Rights League sponsored its annual banquet to coincide with Bufalino's birthday. Bufalino was imprisoned, but that didn't stop more than 750 people from attending. In the same banquet room were mob figures from New York, Philadelphia, Pittsburgh, Binghamton and other cities in the eastern United States mixing with numerous local political figures.

In another telex, dated January 2, 1981, agents noted that the Bufalino family remained heavily involved in the garment and trucking industry and had considerable influence in the Teamsters union. Agents also established that family members were involved in drug trafficking and had considerable influence in Atlantic City's casinos.

Bufalino was released from prison on May 8, 1981, and returned to his Kingston home. But he didn't stay there long and resumed his regular schedule, traveling to New York, Philadelphia, Buffalo and Binghamton for meetings with other organized crime figures. Bufalino was also seen frequently in the company of his old friend Frank Sheeran.

Despite the daily monitoring, the enlistment of confidential sources and the participation of bureaus throughout the country, the RABFAM investigation had yet to bear any fruit in the form of major indictments. The lack of production resulted in an internal dispute within the FBI as to whether the investigation should be shelved.

On September 16, 1981, several FBI departments held a conference to discuss RABFAM and a separate jury tampering case that was being independently prosecuted by a young assistant U.S. attorney, Eric Holder, who worked in the public integrity section. An FBI agent in Scranton told Holder in September 1979 that an informant had alleged that Bufalino underboss James Osticco and several others had bribed a juror in the 1977 flood case involving Louis DeNaples. Holder had learned that the RABFAM investigators had cultivated a confidential informant, and Holder wanted access to the man, who was later identified as Frank Parlopiano, a Scranton man who was introduced to Osticco in 1975 by Russell Bufalino.

Parlopiano had befriended another man, Charles Cortese, in the summer of 1979 and Cortese had confided that he knew Osticco, who had persuaded him to convince his ex-wife to acquit DeNaples and three other men in the 1977 flood trial. Cortese's wife, Rose Ann, was a member of the jury, and her lone vote for a not-guilty verdict led to a hung jury.

Holder wanted immediate access to Parlopiano, arguing that during a recent meeting with Osticco at the Medico headquarters, Parlopiano was forced to strip and searched for any recording devices. Parlopiano's life was in danger, said Holder, and he didn't want to wait until his usefulness to the RABFAM investigators had run out.

Holder was given access to Parlopiano but the RAB-FAM investigation would continue.

Bufalino's next trial once again took place in Manhattan and was again prosecuted by Nathanial Akerman, who had also led the successful federal assault on DePalma and others involved in the Westchester Premier Theater probe.

As Akerman prepared for trial, the Pennsylvania Crime Commission released its latest report, "A Decade of Organized Crime."

The Pennsylvania Crime Commission was formed in the 1970s to investigate and report on the influence of organized crime in Pennsylvania. Made up of attorneys, law enforcement personnel and interested businessman, the commission was one of the few in the United States that regularly reported on organized crime activities. In its latest report, which documented the previous decade, the commission spent considerable time on Russell Bufalino and his Kingston-based family. Aside from documenting Bufalino's lengthy career, the report also identified two-dozen other family members. Among them were Billy D'Elia, Philip Medico and Stephan LaTorre, one of the original Men of Montedoro that had arrived from Sicily at the turn of the century and who, at ninety-four, was still alive and living in Jenkins Township, Luzerne County.

Medico's inclusion came, in part, from the 1979 federal affidavit of former FBI agent John Danary, who had been assigned by J. Edgar Hoover in 1961 to run the New York bureau's criminal-intelligence section. He was assigned to the espionage division from 1966 until his retirement, in 1968, when he became the director of security for the National Football League. It was during his tenure in the espionage division that Danary had access to reports from confidential informants who stated that Philip Medico was a capo in the Bufalino family. Bufalino himself was caught on a secretly recorded tape describing Medico as a capo.

The Pennsylvania Crime Commission report included a photo of Bufalino's modest ranch-style home in Kingston and also revealed that Bufalino had been linked by one of his paid killers, Charles Allen, to two murders, three attempted murders, two attempted arsons and the embezzlement of Teamster funds. Allen, forty-seven, turned government informant following his 1978 arrest on narcotics charges. Allen had made his first hit at age eighteen for Los Angeles mobster Mickey Cohen. He later claimed that he killed a Philadelphia Teamster organizer, Francis Marino in 1976, on orders from Frank Sheeran.

Allen also claimed that Sheeran asked him to dynamite three buildings and rough up four people. The conversation was captured on audiotape by the FBI. Allen also said he went to Medico Industries with Sheeran to collect the dynamite and blasting caps that would be used in the building bombings.

The dynamite was later given to the FBI.

The commission report laid out Bufalino's weekly routine, starting in New York Monday through Wednesday before returning to Pennsylvania and spending Thursday, Friday and Saturday at his office at Medico Industries.

When the trial started, among those called in to testify were Fratianno and Fox, who told their stories to the jury despite frequent interruptions from Bufalino's attorney, Charles Gelso.

When Bufalino took the stand, he spoke about how, since 1942, he had been having lunch at Vesuvio in New York. He said he knew Mike Rizzitello but only casually, and he barely knew James Fratianno, meeting him during a chance encounter at the Rainbow Room. Bufalino said he saw Fratianno again at a restaurant during a trip to Las Vegas and California with his wife, Carrie, in June 1976. Again, that meeting hadn't been planned. Bufalino denied talking about Napoli with Fratianno and denied asking Fratianno to kill Napoli.

As for Steven Fox, Bufalino said he knew Fox from prison and acknowledged that he helped him get a job to obtain his parole. But he never spoke to Fox about Napoli nor did he ever ask Fox to kill Napoli.

Akerman then changed the line of questioning and asked Bufalino about his associations with Carlo Gambino, Angelo Bruno and Vito Genovese and his participation at Apalachin before returning to Napoli.

"Finally, Mr. Bufalino. Let me ask you one question. Did you want to kill Jack Napoli?"

"No."

"Did you ever want to kill Jack Napoli?"

"In a fit of anger in a restaurant, I threatened him, I told him to put the jewels back and stop using my name or I'm going to kill him with my own hands."

"Did you mean it, or were you kidding?"

"No, I wasn't kidding. I was mad. He used my name to rob a jeweler."

After Bufalino stepped down, Akerman received permission from the judge to play the audiotape of Bufalino threatening to kill Napoli. Bufalino was angry, and the man who for more than forty years maintained a quiet dignity in public could be heard angrily spewing how he was going to kill Napoli.

This, said Akerman, was the real Russell Bufalino.

The jury delivered a guilty verdict, and Bufalino was subsequently sentenced to fifteen years in prison. At seventy-eight years old, Russell Bufalino was facing the longest prison term of his life, and there wasn't a politician or police officer that could help him or others he had business with.

A year earlier, representative Daniel Flood was forced to resign from Congress after he pleaded guilty to one count of conspiracy to violate the federal campaign laws for taking cash payoffs. Flood had been charged with taking hundreds of thousands of dollars from assorted lobbyists and contractors. He was acquitted, but the lone holdout juror was later the subject of a jury-tampering investigation. Flood accepted a plea deal prior to a second trial.

Flood also escaped charges that he had steered tens of millions in defense department contracts to Medico Industries. The FBI had wiretapped Medico's offices and captured Bufalino discussing Medico business as well as talking about the Medico brothers and identifying them as members of his crime family. Flood was routinely granted access to the Medico's company jet, but he was never charged in any Bufalino-related business.

And Bufalino underboss James Osticco was facing a lengthy prison term after he was found guilty for fixing the 1977 DeNaples trial. Frank Parlopiano provided the critical testimony, relaying how he had been told that Osticco had approached a member of the jury and bribed her and her husband with $1,000 in cash and a set of tires. The woman was the second juror that Osticco had approached after the jury forewoman declined his advances.

The forewoman died a year later in a mysterious fire.

ON MARCH 23, 1982, attorney Charles Gelso stood before a three-judge panel of the U.S. Court of Appeals, Second Circuit, in Manhattan and argued that his client, Russell Bufalino, had received a bum rap.

Gelso reviewed the details of the case, summarizing how Bufalino allegedly tried in April 1976 to recover a $25,000 debt from Jack Napoli by threatening his life and how, unbeknownst to Bufalino, Napoli had a tape recorder, and the wiretap would be used as evidence to arrest and subsequently convict Bufalino in August 1977. During his four years in prison, Bufalino sought to recruit a prisoner to kill Napoli. Bufalino was later convicted of conspiring to violate the civil rights of a U.S. citizen and endeavoring to obstruct justice. Bufalino was subsequently convicted and sentenced to fifteen years in prison and a $10,000 fine.

Gelso appealed the verdict on several grounds. He argued that evidence, such as the Napoli audiotape, was inadmissible because it was highly prejudicial. The judges concluded that the tape had actually served a double purpose of negating Bufalino's testimony that he never ordered Napoli's murder and also established a motive for killing Napoli.

On June 15, 1982, the court denied his appeal, and now seventy-eight, Bufalino was resigned to spending his golden years inside a federal penitentiary.

# SEVENTEEN

On the morning of January 2, 2008, Pennsylvania State Police troopers Dave Swartz and Rich Weinstock knocked on the door of the residence of the Rev. Joseph Sica. The Catholic priest lived on the grounds of Saint Mary of the Assumption Church, and when he opened his door, he was informed that he was under arrest and charged with perjury for lying about his prior friendship with Russell Bufalino to the grand jury investigating the state Gaming Control Board and Louis DeNaples.

Sica was handcuffed and put in the back of a state police cruiser, but not before the troopers found $1,000 in cash and a handgun in his home. The spiritual advisor and "bodyguard" to Louis DeNaples was distraught. He initially threatened the troopers, saying the new head of security at Mount Airy Casino, Joe Marut had information on both troopers and they would be exposed unless he was released. Merut was a former police major in charge of the Scranton region. The troopers ignored the threats and continued driving down I-81. Sica then asked to use a cell phone.

At Sica's hearing in Harrisburg, Dauphin County first assistant district attorney Fran Chardo described the priest's prior relationship with Russell Bufalino and how Sica had lied to the grand jury about their friendship, which Chardo said could be traced back to the 1970s.

Chardo revisited Sica's appearance before the Dauphin County grand jury in August 2007. The priest wasn't scheduled to testify. But prosecutors were curious about his relationship with DeNaples, and they were downright mesmerized when Billy D'Elia connected Sica to Bufalino, a relationship that Sica later denied during his testimony.

Sica said he had met Bufalino once in the early 1980s, when Bufalino was hospitalized prior to his second prison term. Sica had been visiting the hospital's Catholic patients and happened upon an ailing Bufalino. But D'Elia had already testified that Sica and Bufalino had known each other for years. There were photos, provided by D'Elia, of Bufalino and Sica arm in arm together at Sica's ordination party and at a barbecue soon after. Yet another photo showed Sica at a table embracing Billy D'Elia and Bufalino. Bufalino didn't socialize with just anyone, and his presence clearly indicated a much closer and deeper relationship with Sica and his family.

Sica tried to come to Bufalino's aid following his final conviction, writing letters on Bufalino's behalf seeking his release from prison. Sica even wrote to the wife of Pennsylvania governor Richard Thornburgh, Ginny Thornburgh, on behalf of Bufalino, referring to the mob boss as an innocent man and pleading for her to convince the governor to help "his friend."

It was Chardo who quizzed Sica before the grand jury, and it was those denials about his ties to Bufalino that led to the perjury charge.

*"You didn't know him well, I take it?" said Chardo.*

*"Right," said Sica.*

*"You didn't have any sort of personal relationship with him?"*

*"No."*

*"How many times did you meet Russell Bufalino?"*

*"At the present time I can't really recall."*

*"How long ago would you have met Russell Bufalino for the first time?"*

*"Twenty-six years ago."*

*"Certainly you didn't have any personal relationship with Russell Bufalino?"*

*"No."*

*"Or any member of his family?"*

*"I met his wife, Carrie."*

*"Did you have any personal relationship beyond that with Russell?*

*"No."*

Unbeknownst to Sica, the grand jury had already learned that Bufalino had attended his ordination party, had photos

of Sica and Bufalino and had read a thank-you note Sica had
written to Bufalino and his wife.

> *Dear Russ & Carrie—Words cannot express my thank-*
> *fulness to both of you! You have done a lot for me and you*
> *mean a lot to me. Rest assured of my continued love and*
> *prayers. Love, Joe.*

Standing before the judge wearing his collar and hand-
cuffs, Sica apologized for threatening the troopers following his arrest but otherwise remained mum, following
the instructions given to him earlier during his conversation with DeNaples inside the troopers' car.

While the court was hearing about Sica's alleged relationship with Bufalino, the media began delving into the
priest's past. The *Allentown Morning Call* reported that
Sica had incurred debts that reached $225,000. Most of
the money, nearly $150,000, was owed to the First Na-
tional Community Bank, which DeNaples chaired and
was its largest stockholder.

No one knew how a Roman Catholic priest living on a
paltry $880 per month salary could receive that kind of
credit from a bank. Sica had secured personal loans of
$77,202 and $54,000, and also obtained a $16,500 loan to
buy a 1996 Chevrolet Trailblazer, Eddie Bauer Edition.
Aside from the loans from First National Community
Bank, Sica also managed to obtain a $20,000 personal loan
from LA Bank, a $15,000 personal loan from Community
Bank & Trust Company and a $10,019 credit line from
Associates Investment Company, of Charlotte, North Car-

olina, and he had balances on his Chase and Discover credit cards that totaled $15,176.

Sica had also filed for bankruptcy in March 1997 but later withdrew the filing.

Sica's arrest and the photos of the priest were front-page news and served as a prelude for what everyone now expected would follow—an indictment against Louis De-Naples. The wait wasn't long. On January 30, 2008, DeNaples was charged with four counts of perjury for lying to the gaming board about his ties to Bufalino, D'Elia and two other men.

Ed Marsico delivered the announcement together with state police commissioner Jeffrey Miller inside the capitol building in Harrisburg. According to the findings of fact, the grand jury determined that DeNaples had lied during his testimony under oath about his past relationships with Bufalino, D'Elia and others when he appeared before the gaming board on August 16 and September 28, 2006.

When questioned about D'Elia, DeNaples had simply described him as a local guy who was a customer at First National Community Bank and who from time to time visited DeNaples' auto store to buy car parts. But the grand jury determined there was more to their relationship, one that spanned many years. The transcript from DeNaples' 2006 testimony before gaming investigators was included in the presentment. When quizzed about William D'Elia, his responses were often vague.

*"Do you recognize this person?"*
*"Yes, I do," said DeNaples.*

"How do you know Mr. D'Elia?"

"First of all, he's a local guy that lives in the town not far from us over there and, you know, you hear his name and see him all around. He's a customer at our bank."

"And that bank, you're talking First National?"

"First National Community Bank."

"Okay, and have you ever met him?"

"Yes."

"Okay. And in what circumstances."

"Well, he occasionally was in and out of our parts house to come in there for parts."

"Parts houses?"

"Auto parts."

"Have you spoken to him on the phone as well?"

"Very possibly. He could have called me for something from the bank. That's where his business is with the bank."

"What is the nature of his business?"

"Pardon?"

"What is the nature of his business."

"Well, originally, how he got to our bank is—and this is going back a long, long time ago—he used to work for an appliance house, that the appliance company did business with our bank. That's years ago that he worked for them, and then I believe that he might have bought the business or took over the business. We inherited the account with the bank, the appliance company."'

"You just stated that Mr. D'Elia was at DeNaples Auto Parts. Why would he come to your company?"

"Everybody goes up there. We have a massive automobile dismantling place over there. If you wrecked your car tomorrow and you got a 2006 Mercedes, you could come up and we can get you a door. We have a big operation. We have people from all over the country—rich, poor, professional people. Really, when their cars are broke, they get desperate. They can have the refrigerator broke in the house and the roof leaking but when the car don't run anymore, they panic and come for parts. It's a very big and very elaborate parts, dismantling parts company. There's probably, not to interrupt you, there's probably not a person up in the northeast that didn't once or another visit our auto parts for parts for their cars with their kids or their wife."

"What does Mr. D'Elia do for a living?"

"I have no idea."

"Does Mr. D'Elia have any contracts with Keystone Landfill?"

"No, ma'am."

"Does he have any contracts with any companies that are owned by you?"

"No, ma'am. Whatever contract he might have with the mortgage on a bank."

"Any grievance, any business relationship with Mr. D'Elia?"

"Other than if he came to our counter and bought some parts, that could be years ago."

"You never met with D'Elia on a regular basis?"

"Absolutely not. I told you that if he was in our place a couple of times it was for parts. No—it's all street talk."

The grand jury heard a different story from D'Elia, who testified about DeNaples' attendance at his daughter's wedding. D'Elia also had evidence to prove it—photographs of DeNaples at the reception. D'Elia also told of his closeness to DeNaples' family and how he sat in a hospital with DeNaples' dying father, Patrick. When the elder DeNaples died, D'Elia said Louis gave him his father's rosary beads, saying his father wanted him to have them. The grand jury also heard about the regular meetings between D'Elia and DeNaples at DeNaples' auto parts store and how D'Elia would park in the back and walk in through a private entrance.

Aside from their personal relationship, the grand jury learned that the two men had long-standing business together. D'Elia represented a pay-phone company called BudTel and had obtained permission to place several phones on land or in businesses controlled by DeNaples. One of the phones was placed at DeNaples' auto parts store. Another one was placed on property owned by the Theta Land Corporation, of which DeNaples was a silent partner. D'Elia also set up at least three meetings between BudTel's owner, Barry Shapiro, and DeNaples. In 2001, a folder marked "DeNaples" found in D'Elia's home following a raid by state and federal law enforcement officers revealed other business relationships, including something as innocent as arranging the free printing of brochures for DeNaples' landfill.

The second count of the indictment charged DeNaples with perjury for lying about his past relationship with Russell Bufalino.

From the day he purchased Mount Airy Lodge, in July 2004, until now, no one had ever publicly associated De-Naples with the dead mob boss. All of the stories reported by the media focused on his alleged links to D'Elia. Surprisingly, it was the gaming board's investigators and their attorneys who raised the Bufalino questions to DeNaples during his testimony on August 16, 2006.

*"Are you familiar with Russell Bufalino?"*

*"Only by name," said DeNaples.*

*"B-U-F-A-L-I-N-O. And how do you know him by name?"*

*"Again, he was a local guy, you know, you hear all kinds of newspaper things about him and all."*

*"What kind of things did you hear?"*

*"Well . . ."*

*"In the newspaper or otherwise."*

*"Organized crime or Mafia. I don't know what that is to tell you the truth."*

Through Billy D'Elia's testimony, the grand jury learned that DeNaples and Bufalino knew each other, and well. They too had a long-standing relationship that D'Elia said spanned some thirty years. Once, in the early 1970s, said D'Elia, they were at a prizefight at a local Scranton club when DeNaples complimented Bufalino on a ring he was wearing. Bufalino took the ring off his finger and gave it to DeNaples. On another occasion, following the 1972 flooding from Hurricane Agnes, Bufalino asked DeNaples to repair his wife's Pontiac, which was declared a loss by the insurance company after it was heavily damaged by the storm. DeNaples gave Bufalino the parts to fix the car. He also gave Bufalino two damaged Fiats, which Bufalino, the trained auto mechanic, could combine into one car, which he used for years. Later, in the mid-1970s, Bufalino bought a Cadillac from DeNaples that had been recovered from a theft.

D'Elia told another story about how a fire had gutted DeNaples' home, destroying most of his possessions and clothing. Bufalino sent DeNaples three suits to wear at business meetings. And at the annual Italian American Civil Rights League dinner, DeNaples routinely sat at a table next to Bufalino and his underboss, James Osticco.

DeNaples and Bufalino were clearly close, and the fruits of their relationship resulted in several business interests. DeNaples would often meet with Bufalino's associate Casper "Cappy" Giumento, who, aside from having attended the Apalachin meeting in 1957, had served as a frequent conduit between Bufalino and De-Naples. D'Elia also intimated that DeNaples could point to Bufalino as the reasons for his success, given that no one could have operated a successful landfill or auto parts operation without Bufalino's blessing.

The two other perjury counts were the result of DeNa-ples' denials to the gaming board of his relationships with Shamsud-din Ali, the imprisoned Philadelphia Imam, and Ron White, a Philadelphia attorney, who had since died.

*"How about Clarence Fowler, F-O-W-L-E-R."*

*"No."*

"And I believe he's also Shamsud-din Ali?"

"Do I know him? No, but based on this due diligence for this application over here, it's a possibility that himself and another black person came with a local consultant to our complex to talk about bringing some sludge from Philadelphia to our facility and very, very short conversation. Number one, we don't take sludge. We had no interest in it. That was that kind of thing. I don't even know. I can't tell you—there was two black people and a local consultant who brought them there, a local consultant that lives in the area up by us."

"Who is the local consultant?"

"Brazil, Jamie Brazil. He's a fund-raising guy, local consultant. His father was a—Chairman of the council City of Scranton for years and the brothers are lawyers. So it's a prominent family up in the Scranton area."

"Mr. Brazil brought Ali and—"

"I don't know if it's Ali. It's two black people. That's all I know."

"And it was for the purpose of doing business with sludge and—"

"They wanted—they were interested in bringing sludge to the landfill."

"And that's something you wouldn't do for anybody?"

"We don't take sludge, no. We only take sludge from the local municipality. They got no—we were very in and out, have no interest."

"What year, approximately, did that take place?"

"Four or five years ago, maybe."

"But that's your extent of your contact with him?"

*"I don't know what they were. Like I said, they were two black people."*

*"I'm showing you what is marked as Exhibit 18. It's a photograph. Is that who we're talking about, Mr. Ali?"*

*"Yeah I couldn't—no, I couldn't—"*

*"Maybe it is, maybe it isn't."*

*"To me, black people all look alike."*

Unbeknownst to DeNaples, Ali testified he met with DeNaples as many as four times. The first meeting was at DeNaples' auto parts store, where DeNaples gave Ali a tour of the facility. And despite DeNaples' testimony that he had no interest in sludge, he told Ali was he was receptive and reported his meeting to Billy D'Elia.

According to the indictment, DeNaples had been interviewed prior to his testimony by John Meighan and Roger Greenback, agents from the gaming board's Bureau of Investigations and Enforcement (BIE).

During their investigation, the former FBI agents had learned that DeNaples had received a notice from the U.S. District Court in Philadelphia informing him that he had been captured on a wiretap talking with Ali. When they asked DeNaples about the wiretap, the two BIE agents said he was "vague in his response" and said he "might have received something from the phone company." In fact, on December 19, 2003, DeNaples was personally served with the notice at his office by two FBI agents.

DeNaples was charged with a fourth count of perjury for lying about his relationship with White, who was a close friend of Mayor John F. Street. White had been indicted in 2004 and charged with conspiracy to commit honest services fraud and twenty-two counts of wire fraud. DeNaples denied knowing White, who died while the charges were pending, though the grand jury determined that DeNaples had met with White and Mayor Street in Scranton in 1999. DeNaples later gave White and Street $50,000 but was angered when both men refused to return his phone calls.

DeNaples' arrest spurred the state Gaming Control Board to immediately issue an emergency order suspending DeNaples' gaming license, and management of the casino was turned over to a three-person audit committee. DeNaples was barred from entering his casino. His attorney Richard Sprague called the charges "outrageous." The perjury charges were felonies and could put DeNaples, if convicted, in prison for nearly forty years. The grand jury also called for the gaming board to revoke DeNaples' gaming license and forfeit his $50 million licensing fee.

DeNaples' arrest was condemned by those closest to him, and he immediately drew the support from many of the large institutions that benefited from his charitable endeavors. The Catholic Diocese of Scranton stated, "Mr. DeNaples has generously supported many institutions in the community and many worthwhile endeavors including the Catholic Church, and we are very grateful for his support."

The Community Medical Center Healthcare System reported that "Louis DeNaples has been a great asset to Community Medical Center and the community of

Scranton. His service on our board has been exemplary. I think we all should let due process take its course before passing judgment."

And the University of Scranton, which received millions from DeNaples, including a $35 million student center, stated, "Louis DeNaples and his wife and children are great friends of the University of Scranton. We are grateful for their steadfast support as trustees, alumni, parents, benefactors and volunteers. As always, Louis and his family remain in our prayers."

But the good wishes were tempered by concern over the revelations in the indictment that not only tied De-Naples to Billy D'Elia, but to Russell Bufalino.

DeNaples had seven days to turn himself in, after which he'd have to appear at a preliminary hearing where prosecutors were planning to bring in Billy D'Elia to testify. The mere thought of putting D'Elia in the same room with DeNaples telling the world about DeNaples' ties to organized crime petrified DeNaples' attorneys, who filed an immediate motion with the state supreme court to intervene.

It was an unusual request, but the answer was even more surprising—the court used its Kings Bench authority to intervene in the case and suspended the prosecution pending its review. Kings Bench was the rare use of extraordinary jurisdiction in cases the Supreme Court found to be unusual or grievous. There was nothing unusual or grievous about the DeNaples prosecution other than one of the richest men in Pennsylvania was facing a lengthy term behind bars. But the court stepped in, and its action saved DeNaples from having to face his longtime friend and now nemesis Billy D'Elia.

With the DeNaples case on hold, Dauphin district attorney Ed Marsico was ready to expand his investigations, and he set his sights on other targets. DeNaples had always been the starting point, with the ultimate goal the prosecution of the gaming board and ultimately Governor Ed Rendell and his administration. Testimony before the grand jury supported the theory that the gaming board and Rendell administration had cleared the way for DeNaples to get his slots license. So Marsico impanelled another grand jury with the intent of going after the gaming board's former chairman Tad Decker, with the road potentially leading to Governor Rendell. But since the investigation was tied to the DeNaples case, the Supreme Court order applied, and Marsico was forced to shut down the second grand jury before it heard from a single witness.

JUST A MONTH later, in May 2008, the League of Women Voters of Pennsylvania filed a federal lawsuit claiming that Governor Ed Rendell made a secret deal with the state Supreme Court to gain the court's support of gaming legislation. The suit specifically claimed that former chief justice Ralph Cappy had an agreement with Rendell and several high-ranking lawmakers to support the state in any gaming cases that came before the court in return for judicial pay raises.

Filed in the Middle District in Harrisburg, the lawsuit alleged the agreement violated the league's constitutional rights to due process since the league was one of the groups that filed a previous lawsuit that challenged the constitutionality of the state's slots laws. In that case, the Supreme Court sided with Rendell against the league by ruling in June 2005 that the gaming law, Act 71, was constitutional.

Just two weeks later, on July 7, the general assembly approved a pay increase for all members of the legislative and judicial branches of government. The pay hike struck a nerve with a public that rarely paid much attention to any of the shenanigans occurring in Harrisburg. The public was so incensed over the pay raises that it forced the legislature to act to cancel the increases. But the Supreme Court justices ignored the public and kept its raise and those of more than one thousand other judges throughout Pennsylvania.

The details of the lawsuit were astonishing. In May 2006, an unidentified state senator made the initial allegation that several members of the court made the deal with Rendell and legislative leaders. The account was confirmed by other unidentified lawmakers. Paul Rossi, the attorney representing the league, said in the lawsuit that the court initially began its corruptive quid pro quo with Republican legislators back in the 1990s and negotiated its decisions with lawmakers who sought rulings on certain cases before the court.

The lawsuit also alleged that two other Supreme Court justices, Ronald D. Castille and Michael Eakin, were spotted leaving a closed-door meeting at then majority leader

Sam Smith's office just a few weeks before the gaming legislation was passed.

Smith denied the allegation, saying it was ridiculous since he was an opponent of the slots bill. Castille called the suit "outrageous."

This wasn't the first time the Supreme Court had been accused of being corrupt, which on the face of it was an astounding charge against the state's highest legal authority. Word was also filtering down that Denyse Miskin, who headed the gaming board's Bureau of Corporate Compliance and Internal Controls, was privately telling associates about an incident at a dinner just days before the slots licenses were awarded. Several people were questioning the suitability of Louis DeNaples and how, on an expected appeal from one of the losing applicants, the court would confirm the board's decision to give him a license.

Miskin's story was stunning. She said that board chairman Tad Decker took out his cell phone and, in front of less than a dozen gaming board executives, called one of the justices.

"I'm trying to reassure members of my staff that you will support any decision we make on gaming licenses," said Decker.

"Of course," said a male a voice on the other end of the phone, affirming what Decker had said. Decker put the phone away.

"See, we have nothing to worry about," he allegedly said.

As events unfolded, the court did nothing to disprove the allegations that it cut a deal with the Rendell administration, as it remained a thorn in the side of Ed Marsico.

For the next year, Marsico and his deputy Fran Chardo negotiated with DeNaples' attorneys, with the ever-present shadow of the court hanging over those discussions. They finally reached an agreement on April 14, 2009, when Marsico dropped the perjury charges against DeNaples in return for DeNaples agreeing to give up ownership of Mount Airy. The casino would be transferred to his daughter, Lisa, though DeNaples would retain a financial interest in Mount Airy as the guarantor of $250 million in financing he had received from JP Morgan Chase.

DeNaples, who also agreed to pay for the cost of the prosecution, issued a statement, saying, "I am relieved and gratified that the district attorney has recognized that the criminal charges against me are baseless. I have said from the start that I am innocent, and that's the truth. I have said from the start that I have no contact with organized crime, and that's the truth. I am glad that we have finally put these issues to rest."

The charges pending against the Rev. Joseph Sica were also dropped.

Marsico's consideration of a plea deal for DeNaples was first broached to the state police during a meeting the week before the announcement. Marsico explained that the Supreme Court had interfered in his case twice already, and he feared that no matter what he did, the court would see to it that the DeNaples prosecution would never move forward. The court's use of its Kings Bench authority in a simple perjury case was unusual at best, said Marsico, and at worst downright suspect. But there was nothing he could do, and given the unrelenting pressure by the court and by DeNaples' attorney Richard Sprague, who seemed to have the court's ear, reaching a plea agreement and getting DeNaples out of gaming, at least on paper, was the next best result.

Sprague had been a thorn in Marsico's side since the perjury charges were filed. The aging attorney, now in his eighties, had an illustrious legal history, having served in the Philadelphia district attorney's office from 1958 to 1974 and finishing up his last eight years there as the first assistant district attorney. It was during his tenure in the district attorney's office that he met other notable figures, including Ed Rendell and Supreme Court justice Ronald Castille.

In 1976, Sprague was appointed chief counsel to the Church Committee and was on the inside of the new probe into the assassination of John F. Kennedy and the CIA's assassination attempts on world leaders, including Cuba's Fidel Castro. Sprague had assembled a large staff of attorneys, researchers and investigators, but his tenure was marked by one controversy after another, including his battles with the CIA over demands for sensitive information, which were universally rejected. Sprague was forced to resign from the committee in 1978, and over the course of the next thirty years, he would become one of the most powerful and influential attorneys in Pennsylvania.

In 1990, he was awarded $24 million in a successful libel suit he filed against the *Philadelphia Inquirer* stemming from articles in 1973 that questioned whether he failed to prosecute a 1963 murder case as a favor to a friend.

Coincidently, while defending DeNaples, Sprague had an interest in a Philadelphia casino, SugarHouse, and a new lobbying firm, the Pennsylvania Casino Association, which had engaged former State Supreme Court justice Stephen Zappala Jr. to lobby on its behalf. Zappala was paid more than $500,000, but it wasn't clear exactly who or what he was lobbying.

The funding for the casino group was provided by Louis DeNaples.

The state police were furious with Marsico and vehemently argued to continue the prosecution. The police had spent five years probing gaming, and its best witness, Billy D'Elia, had yet to sit in a courtroom and tell the world all he knew about Louis DeNaples. For his cooperation, D'Elia had been sentenced in November 2008 to serve nine years in federal prison after pleading guilty to money laundering and witness tampering. He had faced up to thirty years. His attorney, James Swetz, sought a reduced sentence, given D'Elia's cooperation in the De-Naples case, but the judge believed nine years was short enough.

Federal prosecutors couldn't have been happier.

"The sentencing of William D'Elia comes after a series of carefully coordinated investigations conducted by state and federal law enforcement agencies, including the Federal Bureau of Investigation, the Department of Homeland Security, Immigration and Customs Enforcement, the Internal Revenue Service–Criminal Investigation Division, the Pennsylvania State Police and the U.S. Department of Labor," said U.S. attorney Martin Carlson. "Today's sentencing sends a powerful message about the commitment of law enforcement to break the grip of organized crime . . . and to ensure that the people . . . can live free of the influence of organized criminal figures."

John P. Kelleghan, special agent in charge of the Immigration and Customs Enforcement office of investigations in Philadelphia, commended the Pennsylvania State Police and FBI for dismantling a "long-standing criminal enterprise."

"With the sentencing of William D'Elia today, we close a chapter on the Bufalino organized crime family and its leadership. Thanks to the collaborative efforts of all the agencies involved, we have dismantled an organization that has exploited our community for decades," Kelleghan said.

But Marsico was firm, even against the objections of Chardo, who supported the police in their argument to roll the dice and allow a jury to decide DeNaples' fate. To that end, Chardo never once believed the case would ever be tried. DeNaples would certainly agree to a different set of plea terms before engaging in such a spectacle, but Marsico firmly believed that the Supreme Court would again find a way to interfere with the prosecution. Marsico was resigned that DeNaples had the support of the court, as he did Ed Rendell.

The governor had remained strangely quiet throughout the entire DeNaples prosecution. He once hailed De-Naples as a "salt of the earth" kind of guy, but he refrained from making any public comments until the plea deal was announced.

"When Mr. DeNaples was charged every newspaper in the state editorialized about how this was so bad and showed a weakness in the gaming law. But now that the charges have been dropped, what does that stand for?" said Rendell. "I happen to know Mr. DeNaples, and I know him well. He had a run-in with the law years ago but he's been a good citizen, and you can ask any charity or community or civic association, and they will tell you that. He's licensed by the U.S. banking department to be a banker. I don't think that the charges were dropped will be bad for Pennsylvania."

Rendell never addressed the hundreds of thousands in campaign contributions he received from DeNaples, his associates and business partners. Nor did Rendell address the allegations in the League of Women Voters lawsuit.

The FBI and state police knew about the contributions and believed the money was being funneled from DeNaples to Rendell, but their review in 2007 ended quietly.

Although DeNaples himself was technically out of gaming, his family still owned the casino, which had been DeNaples' plan all along. Now approaching seventy, De-Naples intended to leave Mount Airy under the control of his children, so the plea result merely moved his plans ahead a few years.

What DeNaples did not expect was to lose his

Dunmore-based bank. He had served as a director at First National Community Bank since 1972 and over the years became its largest stockholder and chairman. After the perjury charges were filed, the bank's regulator, the Office of Comptroller of Currency (OCC) in Washington, D.C., took action to permanently separate DeNaples, saying that it was required to prohibit anyone who had agreed to "enter into a pretrial diversion or similar program" from any involvement, including working, owning or controlling, a national bank. In effect, since the perjury charges stemmed from allegations that DeNaples lied about his organized crime contacts, he did not meet that standard set by the OCC.

DeNaples fought the ban, arguing that he never admitted to having organized crime contacts, and filed a federal lawsuit against the OCC seeking reinstatement. But the suit was dismissed by U.S. District Judge Thomas I. Vanskie in February 2010, who ruled that the OCC and not the federal courts had jurisdiction over the case.

DeNaples subsequently filed an appeal with the Third Circuit Court of Appeals in Philadelphia, but again he was rebuffed. DeNaples was subsequently ordered to divest himself of all interests in the bank, including the sale of his shares.

While DeNaples fought for his interests in the bank, regulators swarmed over the bank's books, looking for evidence of lax lending practices and suspicious transactions. For years, First National had been a source of easy money for a host of people close to DeNaples and other bank officers. Billy D'Elia had accounts there, as did

DeNaples' constant companion, the Rev. Joseph Sica, who on his paltry salary somehow was approved for tens of thousands in loans. Through the years numerous businesses, knowing they wouldn't be approved elsewhere, turned to First National. The terms were usually onerous, and failure to pay meant foreclosure, as was the case with the Pocmont Resort in the Poconos. After undergoing a multimillion-dollar renovation with financing from First National, the resort defaulted on its debt, and the bank took over the note.

When bank regulators finished their probe, they imposed heavy restrictions after concluding the bank had for years conducted unsafe and unsound banking practices. The bank had, as suspected, failed to maintain internal controls and failed to report suspicious transactions that led to huge losses over the past few years, including millions in bad loans. One loan that defaulted, for $4 million, was for a land project guaranteed by two board members. The bank had also been implicated in a burgeoning scandal involving two Luzerne County judges accused of taking cash payoffs for sentencing teenagers to a private juvenile detention facility in Pittston Township.

The case, known as "Kids for Cash," shocked even the most jaded observers following local corruption. Lackawanna County Judges Michael Conahan and Mark Ciavarella were approved for loans from the bank to establish a depository in Florida that took the payoffs from the scheme. The bank also financed the judges' purchase of a Florida condominium. Conahan was a member of the bank's board from 2003 until his resignation in 2009.

Federal prosecutors credited Billy D'Elia for alerting them to the scam.

For DeNaples, the loss of the bank was perhaps the biggest blow throughout the entire casino saga, and his reputation suffered. From the day he purchased Mount Airy, in 2004, the usually quiet and publicity-shy businessman was front-page news. And as the evidence mounted against him, the sting and embarrassment to himself and his family was something he never envisioned.

In May 2009, the state police took one more shot at prosecuting the Katrina truck investigation. The case had originally been transferred to the police from the U.S. attorney's office in Scranton after the FBI determined that the issue over titling was a state matter. The department's Bureau of Criminal Investigations, which was assisting with the DeNaples probe, took on the Katrina investigation, and with the help of Dauphin County prosecutors, the case was referred to Lackawanna County for prosecution since that was where the trucks had been sold.

But district attorney Andy Jarbola declined to investigate, saying a local state police barracks, Troop R, already took a look at the matter and determined there was no wrongdoing.

Police commanders in Harrisburg, who supported the Dauphin County effort, had no idea what Jarbola was talking about, and their reaction was, "What investigation?"

"We never heard about [the Troop R] investigation," said a police spokesman, who believed that Troop R would never have been allowed to probe DeNaples, given the Dunmore barracks was in DeNaples' hometown and, more important, the commanding officer there, Major Joe Marut, had been captured on police surveillance video visiting DeNaples at his auto parts business. Because of his close contact with DeNaples, police brass would never have allowed Marut's involvement in a DeNaples probe. Marut had also, coincidently, retired and taken a position with DeNaples as Mount Airy Casino's chief of security.

Although DeNaples avoided additional prosecution, several of those invoked in the gaming legislation found themselves finally answering to law enforcement for other crimes. Former senator Vince Fumo was serving a five-year term for corruption, while Senator Robert Mellow resigned after word leaked that he was now under investigation. Federal agents had raided his office and home in June 2010 and removed boxes of documents in what they said was an ongoing public corruption probe. Mellow later pleaded guilty to conspiracy and was sentenced in November 2012 to eighteen months in prison. Meanwhile, state senator Raphael Musto was indicted for allegedly taking nearly $40,000 in kickbacks for his help in getting a company state grants and funding. Musto hailed from Pittston.

# EIGHTEEN

Though Dauphin County district attorney Ed Marsico's grand jury probe ended in 2009, the information gathered from his investigation was quietly given to the state attorney general, Tom Corbett, who was preparing to empanel a grand jury of his own.

It would be six months before the public learned of the statewide grand jury in Pittsburgh, which was probing whether the gaming board steered gaming licenses to DeNaples and several other licensees. The *Pittsburgh Post-Gazette* was the first to report the new grand jury after learning that gaming board records had been subpoenaed. Governor Ed Rendell was quick to say that he believed the gaming board did a "solid job" and denied there was any political influence exerted to decide the outcomes.

Dozens of witnesses were subpoenaed to testify, several

of whom had previously testified in front of the DeNaples grand jury. It took two years for the state prosecutors to complete their work, and on May 19, 2011, they released their findings.

The report was a shocking yet sobering document that laid out, in detail, the problems that dodged gaming from its creation and all but confirmed the original fears of former deputy police commissioner Ralph Periandi. There was, as he suspected, a scheme to benefit several applicants, among them Louis DeNaples.

The grand jury report, in one of its chief findings, didn't mince words, saying the "[Gaming] Board took the public policy objectives and essentially turned them on their head."

The report was detailed and began even before the gaming legislation was approved, on July 4, 2004. The grand jury, for instance, learned that Senator Mellow approached William Conaboy, a Scranton attorney, to tell him he would be Mellow's choice to serve on the soon-to-be-created gaming board.

Conaboy testified that he was told that Louis DeNaples would most likely apply for a gaming license. Conaboy said he expressed concern since he was not only friends with DeNaples, but was also one of his attorneys. They also served together on the board of Allied Health Services, which Conaboy also represented. Conaboy said he told Mellow he could not vote on anything related to DeNaples. Nevertheless, after the legislation passed in July 2004, Conaboy was appointed to the board by Mellow, as promised, to a part-time position that paid $145,000 per year.

Conaboy testified that Mellow told him before his official acceptance on the board that "he was only going to say it one time, that he was saying it then because I was not on the Board as of that date, he said his interest was solely his senatorial district, and if that applicant was qualified and met all the requirements of the Gaming Act, that he would like to see a casino in his district."

The applicant would be DeNaples, and the grand jury found that BIE's background investigation of Louis DeNaples, at least initially, was moot. The grand jury relayed how, less than two weeks after the gaming legislation was passed, in July 2004, DeNaples formed a limited liability company, Mt. Airy LLC, and set his sights on gaining a Category 2 slots license, which allowed for up to 5,000 slot machines.

But DeNaples didn't even own the Mount Airy property, a purchase that would not be completed until December 2004. DeNaples later broke ground on Mount Airy in July 2006, a full six months *before* he was awarded a gaming license. The report quoted a BIE agent who opined, "You would have to be, I guess, pretty rich or pretty sure that you were going to get a license if you were going to do that."

The grand jury said the DeNaples application had been guided and massaged to approval, with board members and other officials personally interfering with BIE's background report. David Kwait, BIE's director, testified about a chance encounter with DeNaples during a hearing in Philadelphia.

"I was standing with one of the commissioners and a couple of agents and either Conaboy or (Ray) Angeli, and I think it would have had to be Conaboy, come over and said, 'Hey, I want you to meet Louie DeNaples.' . . . I got to shake Louis DeNaples' hand, and he asked me a question. He said 'Who could I get? What company could I get to do a background investigation of me that would satisfy you and the queen?' And I said, 'What?' And he asked me again, and I really didn't respond to him. Later, Conaboy pushed and said, 'Well, suggest one,' and I suggested, 'Well, try the Kroll Agency in New York,' and that was the end of my one and only conversation with Louis DeNaples."

When asked if he was bothered that a current commissioner was introducing him to an applicant, Kwait replied, "Yes." Kwait was also asked if the notion that DeNaples would need to hire an outside agency to vouch for him seemed a bit odd.

"For sure," he said.

"If he has nothing to hide, shouldn't he just be able to rely on your own agency to give him a clean bill of health?" asked a prosecutor.

"Hopefully, I agree 100 percent, so it was nonsense to begin with. No matter who he hired to do whatever, it wouldn't have made a hill of beans as we proceeded to do our job."

The grand jury learned that BIE's initial background report included some damning information, including portions of the 2001 federal affidavit that quoted confidential informants relaying business ties between DeNaples and Billy D'Elia. The report also included a copy of the 2006 federal search warrant of D'Elia's home and car, where state police and the U.S. Department of Homeland Security found DeNaples' unlisted home number in D'Elia's address book. They also found D'Elia's bank statements from First National Community Bank in Dunmore.

BIE's initial background report also included the Katrina truck investigation, along with reports from the old Pennsylvania Crime Commission. Of particular interest were the details of how four people, including Bufalino crime family underboss James Osticco, had tampered with the DeNaples federal jury during his 1977 trial for fleecing the federal government for cleanup work from Hurricane Agnes.

The grand jury learned that DeNaples' ties to imprisoned Philadelphia cleric Shamsud-din Ali and his presence at the 1999 wedding of D'Elia's daughter with organized crime figures from Philadelphia, including "Skinny" Joe Merlino, were eventually deleted from BIE's final report.

To put the gaming board's actions in perspective, other gaming jurisdictions, such as Nevada and New Jersey, would never have deleted damning information from an investigative report, even if it was deemed hearsay. The applicant in those states must prove his suitability. That wasn't the case in Pennsylvania, said the grand jury, even after BIE made no less than four criminal referrals to other agencies, including the FBI and state police. One of those referrals concerned the FBI wiretap of Shamsud-din Ali, while others referred to the Katrina trucks and political contributions from RAM Consultants, a DeNaples entity.

As for information that made it into the report, much of it was whitewashed.

For instance, the report relayed how BIE agent Roger Greenback sought to investigate the vendors and construction contractors building the new Mount Airy hotel and casino but failed to get Mount Airy to cooperate. A casino attorney, Joe Wright, wrote to the board saying Mount Airy would not respond to any requests for information from BIE. That simple denial to cooperate was enough to deny DeNaples and Mount Airy a license, argued Greenback.

Mount Airy officials also complained to the gaming board that they believed they were being "picked on." It was Tad Decker, the board chairman, who brought Greenback in to hear a simple message: lay off Mount Airy.

Concerned over the inappropriate interference, Greenback subsequently transferred the Mount Airy background investigation to the central BIE office, in Harrisburg. But that didn't stop the board from completely changing the final DeNaples background report, which the grand jury found "were no reflection of the real investigative facts developed by BIE and were further tainted by the applicants editing through threat of litigation."

"Significant information" was removed from Mount Airy's BIE report, along with two other casino applicants, among them Don Barden, who was approved for a casino in Pittsburgh. Barden was the only African-American awarded a casino license, and his selection was the completion of the deal with the legislative black caucus in Philadelphia for its support of the gaming initiative. According to the grand jury report, Barden, like DeNaples, "received (his) fair share of preferential or special treatment."

One licensing attorney testified that gaming board members were "horse trading" their votes, agreeing to vote for each other's favored applicants prior to the actual hearings. In effect, the gaming board members weren't voting for their favored applicant but for the favorite of the person who appointed them, either a legislative leader or Rendell.

As for Barden, he was based in Detroit and was the owner of several casinos in the Midwest through his Majestic Star company. Barden, like DeNaples, was a self-made man who, on paper, had a net worth that reached into the hundreds of millions. In reality, Barden was a financial nightmare whose background investigative report was, like DeNaples', completely scrubbed. The final BIE report on Barden had been whittled down to twenty-nine pages from eighty and omitted lengthy passages on Barden's history and his gambling habits. The original report included information on how Barden, during the first quarter of 2005, wrote checks to five casinos to cover personal gambling losses of more than $500,000. Barden also had outstanding markers, or gambling debts, of nearly $2 million. Over a five-year span, from 2001 to

2006, Barden lost more than $11 million while gambling, yet none of that made it into his final investigative report.

Aside from his BIE investigative report, other checks on Barden were also altered, including his financial suitability report, which originally came in at six and one-half pages and included details of previous financial performance, his financial risk profile and an analysis of his individual financial worth and projection of his performance should he gain a license. In fact, there was a comment within the report that said that "the Majestic Star Casino, LLC, has demonstrated weak financial performance during the fiscal years ended December 31, 2000 through and including December 31, 2005."

Barden's final report was two and one-half pages and didn't include any financial analysis; instead, the whole project was based on a promise by the New York bank Jefferies & Co. to fund the $435 million project with a commitment letter. The entire project was, in reality, completely leveraged.

After receiving his gaming license, Barden's Majestic Star quickly ran into financial trouble during construction, and Barden was eventually forced to sell the casino. Barden died of lung cancer in May 2011 at age sixty-seven.

Perhaps most incredible, the grand jury found that attorneys for Mount Airy were allowed to review drafts of DeNaples' suitability reports up to three weeks before he would sit for his closed-door hearings, while his chief competitor, Pocono Manor, received two days to review their documents. Ideally, gaming investigators would file their reports, which would then be reviewed by their superiors and BIE attorneys. Upon completion, the background report is then submitted to the gaming board members for their review. Instead, the grand jury found that the process in Pennsylvania saw BIE submit a background report that, when submitted to the board, had been completely edited and was devoid of any damning information. In other words, said the grand jury, the fix was in, and DeNaples, as expected, got his license.

According to the grand jury report, Mount Airy was treated differently "almost from the start." The grand jury intimated but couldn't decide if this was "because the potential suitability issues were known or because this was a critically important license from a political standpoint."

The BIE investigation had revealed, according to the report, "significant areas of concern regarding the character, honesty, and integrity of Louis DeNaples," and it cited his 1978 felony conviction, the Katrina truck case, his political contributions and suspected ties to organized crime. The investigators also testified as to how "disappointed" they were that DeNaples received a license. Some were more disappointed, while others, according to the grand jury, expressed "outright disbelief, anger and embarrassment." David Kwait, the former head of BIE, said the DeNaples case was "what not to do in a gaming situation."

In their defense, gaming board members explained that they didn't consider DeNaples' felony conviction because it occurred outside the fifteen-year statute that was included in the gaming legislation. They also dismissed the political contributions and Katrina truck incident because "no one brought charges" against DeNaples. Remarkably, they said they didn't believe any of the allegations were considered an "issue of bad character, honesty, or integrity for DeNaples to overcome." The threshold for bad character was a criminal conviction, they said.

Ken McCabe, the former FBI agent, agreed that he couldn't consider DeNaples' previous felony conviction.

During the suitability hearings, which occurred over three consecutive nights, DeNaples was protected not just by his own attorneys, but by the gaming board itself. The board's chief counsel, Frank Donaghue, limited the questioning of witnesses to just several minutes.

The grand jury also relayed how a gaming board attorney, Don Shiffer, took a keen interest in the DeNaples investigation.

Shiffer was an attorney from Scranton who had gained his job with the help of former board member William Conaboy (who had been appointed to the board by Robert Mellow), so it wasn't lost on anyone that Shiffer would have an interest in Mount Airy's license.

In an odd quirk, Shiffer was actually assigned to work as the licensing attorney for Mount Airy's chief competitor, Pocono Manor. Despite having a larger facility, higher gaming-revenue estimates and a world-class gaming executive, Dennis Gomes, to serve as its president, Pocono Manor was not in Mellow's senatorial district and was thus directly competing with DeNaples.

Once he arrived, Shiffer immediately requested that he be reassigned to work the Mount Airy application, and he even stated that he knew a few people involved with

Mount Airy. After his request was denied, Shiffer approached another attorney, Lisa McClain, who was working the Mount Airy application and asked if she would be willing to swap applicants. McLain said no. Shiffer nevertheless interjected himself in the Mount Airy application process, requesting to see drafts of DeNaples' suitability report and at times making the requests claiming to be the licensing attorney assigned to Mount Airy.

On another occasion, McLain testified how she couldn't locate a box of documents relating to the Mount Airy application. Acting on a hunch, she went to Shiffer's office and found them under his desk. Near the end of the DeNaples licensing review, Shiffer again asked to work on the Mount Airy application and was given the task of vetting several paragraphs of information relating to key employees, including DeNaples' daughter Lisa.

Shiffer was invited by Ray Angeli, the board member appointed by Mellow to replace William Conaboy after Conaboy's 2006 resignation, to attend DeNaples closed-door suitability hearings as an advisor. Angeli was the president of Lackawanna College, where DeNaples' brother Dominick served as a board member, and was yet another lackey appointed to help along the DeNaples application.

During the suitability hearings, Shiffer was seen writing notes to Angeli and whispering in his ear, but his presence was seen as a conflict by others, given he was responsible for the Pocono Manor report.

"Everybody knew he was there for Louie DeNaples," said Kwait and others.

Near the end of the hearing, Shiffer approached board chairman Tad Decker and complained that BIE was "dirtying up" DeNaples and favoring Pocono Manor. Decker called over to Kwait.

"Is it true that you weren't properly investigating Pocono Manor? Instead you were trying to dirty up Louie DeNaples?"

Kwait testified that he looked at Shiffer and said, "Did you say that to him? You are too fucking close to this DeNaples thing."

Decker had a somewhat different recollection of the incident. During his testimony, he said he recalled DeNaples testifying to alleged violations regarding campaign contributions and the Katrina trucks.

"And what we got—what happened is Ray—I think it was Ray, could have been Shiffer, said to me, 'Why are we spending so much time on DeNaples? It isn't really fair.' And then I said, listen, the guy pled nolo to a crime how many years ago, 17, 18, 25 years ago, whatever it was, I forget to be honest. I said, we have a duty to do that and also we have these issues with people complaining about Katrina trucks or, you know, something else. I said, we're here to investigate. And the response was, we spent—and I think it's probably true—we spent more time on DeNaples than we did on everyone else combined. I don't know if that's true or not, but that was kind of what was said back. And then Shiffer and I sort of got into an argument about it.

"Shiffer would eventually leave the board for private

practice, and within a month, he took a job with a Scranton law firm, Wright and Reihner, and was assigned to an office inside Mount Airy to represent the firm and the casino. In essence, said the grand jury, Shiffer was rewarded by becoming Mount Airy's de facto in-house counsel, and the grand jury determined that Shiffer's employment with Wright and Reihner was "a subterfuge to hide the fact that he left the Board to work immediately for Mount Airy."

In October 2008, Shiffer was formally hired by Mount Airy as its general counsel and, subsequently, a vice president.

As a key employee, Shiffer had to submit to a background investigation, and the report revealed that Shiffer's connections to Mount Airy ran deep during his tenure with the gaming board. Cell phone records showed that he made ninety-one calls to Lisa DeNaples and three hundred calls to Ray Angeli, which the grand jury found to be significant. In examining the calls, the grand jury found that Shiffer spoke with Lisa DeNaples during supposedly private gaming board executive sessions and board meetings and following a state Supreme Court ruling that Pocono Manor could use certain exhibits as they appealed the denial of their license.

Shiffer claimed that he had developed a professional friendship with Lisa DeNaples and that he simply made himself available to her to answer questions. But the grand jury found that Shiffer's contact with both DeNaples and Angeli was significant and enough to "raise serious questions about the integrity of the process." In effect, Louis DeNaples had his own attorney spying for him inside the gaming board.

Further in its report, the grand jury revealed that at least one board member was prepared to vote against the DeNaples application. Despite the direct evidence involving the Katrina trucks and political contributions and alleged ties to organized crime during his December 2006 closed-door suitability hearings, DeNaples was found suitable for a slots license. With the final vote approaching, board member Ken McCabe told BIE's David Kwait and Roger Greenback that he needed something concrete on DeNaples so he could vote against Mount Airy.

Greenbank subsequently gave McCabe a report on a Scranton-area businessman, Frank Pavlico, who had been charged in the money-laundering case that snared Billy D'Elia. During interviews with BIE, Pavlico said he was D'Elia's cousin and was all too familiar with the lengthy business and personal relationship between D'Elia and DeNaples. Some of the information reported by Pavlico relayed business and family events D'Elia and DeNaples attended together, including meetings with other members of organized crime.

The Pavlico interview had been excluded from DeNaples' suitability report after the board determined it was secondhand information, but McCabe got a copy. In addition, Greenbank contacted D'Elia's attorney, James Swetz, requesting an interview with D'Elia, who was being held without bail in a Pike County prison after he was charged in October 2006 in a superseding indictment with conspiring to murder a witness in his money-laundering case.

D'Elia fired his attorney Philip Gelso, and the courts appointed Swetz to represent D'Elia. Swetz subsequently told Greenbank to contact the U.S. attorney's office, but it declined the interview request. BIE, as federal, state and local prosecutors had warned, was a civilian agency, and criminal information could only be shared with other law enforcement agencies. Without D'Elia, and with a warning by gaming board counsel Frank Donaghue to toe the line, McCabe reluctantly voted to award the license to DeNaples and Mount Airy.

Despite its damning and eye-opening report, the grand jury did not recommend criminal charges. Instead, it recommended a laundry list of necessary changes to state gaming law.

Greg Fajt, the former secretary of the Department of Revenue who now served as the gaming board chairman, saw the report as a victory and proudly proclaimed that, in his words, "no one was indicted."

# NINETEEN

The disappearance of Jimmy Hoffa remained a mystery and the subject of countless investigations, grand juries, books and movies and yet another FBI review in 2003.

It wasn't until 2004 when Frank Sheeran, then eighty-four years old and seeking to make his peace with God, finally confessed to killing Hoffa to author Charles Brandt, who told Sheeran's story in his book, *I Heard You Paint Houses*.

Sheeran had long been one of the FBI's prime suspects, along with Bufalino, Tony Provenzano, Sally Briguglio, Anthony Giancala and brothers Steve and Tom Andretta, only prosecutors never had enough evidence to charge them.

For his part, Sheeran said he never knew who, aside from Bufalino, had planned Hoffa's murder. He had attended a meeting in New York at Bufalino's Vesuvio restaurant several days after Hoffa disappeared with Bufalino, Provenzano and several others. All seemed relieved that Hoffa was gone, he said.

It was just a week earlier when Sheeran said he and Bufalino were driving with their wives to Detroit to attend the wedding of Bill Bufalino's daughter when they dropped the women off at a diner near Lake Erie in Port Clinton, Ohio, under the premise they had some business to take care of. Russell always had stops to make, so this one wasn't unusual. After leaving the women, Bufalino and Sheeran then drove to a commuter airport with a grass airstrip, where a small, single-engine plane was waiting to take Sheeran to Detroit, which was about one hundred miles away.

Sheeran said nothing to the pilot, and an hour later, the plane landed at an airfield in Pontiac, which was north of Detroit. Waiting for Sheeran was a gray Ford with the keys under the mat, and he drove into Detroit to a nondescript brick house in a quiet neighborhood. When Sheeran walked inside the house, he saw Sally "Bugs" Briguglio and the Andretta brothers. All were waiting for Chuckie O'Brien.

The plan that was conceived was for O'Brien, Sheeran and Sally Bugs to drive to the Red Fox restaurant to pick up Hoffa and then bring him back to the house. Seeing O'Brien, who had been raised by Hoffa, and Sheeran together was designed to put Hoffa at ease. Only O'Brien had no idea as to the plot that was about to unfold.

O'Brien, Sheeran and Sally Bugs drove to the restaurant and saw an obviously irritated Hoffa walking to his green Pontiac. Hoffa had been waiting hours for Provenzano and Giacalone and believed he had been stood up. When he saw O'Brien pull up, he was furious and didn't hide his feelings when he was introduced to Sally Briguglio, who said he was with Provenzano.

When Hoffa began questioning O'Brien and Briguglio, he looked inside the car and saw Sheeran. Briguglio said his "friend" wanted to be at the meeting. Sheeran explained his tardiness by saying there were delays getting to Detroit, but he was here now with his "friend," whom Hoffa knew was Bufalino.

Seeing O'Brien and Sheeran quieted Hoffa, and he dropped his guard and got into the maroon Mercury. When they pulled up to the house, only Sheeran and Hoffa would leave the car. As O'Brien drove away with Briguglio, Hoffa walked just ahead of Sheeran up the stairs, through the front door and into a small vestibule.

Hoffa expected to see several men there, including Bufalino, Provenzano and Giacalone. Instead, the house was empty, and Hoffa knew what was about to happen. He immediately turned around to reach for the door, but Sheeran had pulled out his gun and shot him twice in the back of the head.

Sheeran calmly walked out of the house and got into the gray Ford, and he drove back to the airstrip in Pontiac, where the plane was waiting. When he arrived back in Port Clinton, Bufalino was still there in Sheeran's black Lincoln. They picked up their wives and drove to Detroit for the wedding.

Sheeran learned later from Bufalino that the Andretta

brothers were the "cleaners" who tidied up the house and took Hoffa's body to a nearby incinerator, where it was cremated. They then picked up Sally Briguglio and flew to New Jersey.

The plan to kill Jimmy Hoffa was carried out with precision. Years later, after Sheeran's 2004 confession, questions followed. To investigators, the press and inquisitive public that for years sought resolution, it was a cut-and-dried case of Hoffa infuriating his organized crime partners, who responded in their typical and extremely prejudicial fashion.

But there was another theory, one that was originally suggested by, of all people, William Bufalino, who said in 1978 that he believed that the CIA was involved and that Hoffa was quieted because he was scheduled to testify before the Church Committee.

And it wasn't so much that anyone feared Hoffa would talk about underworld figures but that he would connect certain people to assassination plots against Fidel Castro, and possibly provide information about the assassination of President John F. Kennedy.

Russell Bufalino never believed Hoffa would talk. But when he saw his own name splashed across the *Time* magazine article, Bufalino didn't wait. He had long relied on a simple saying he once had framed: "There is no conspiracy when only one remains."


RUSSELL BUFALINO TOILED in the federal prison in Danbury for eight years. Despite his incarceration, he maintained firm control over his family into the late 1980s, sending orders through Billy D'Elia.

In Bufalino's absence, D'Elia had become the undeniable star of the family, and his rapid ascent was noted by the FBI in their RABFAM reports.

"D'Elia has emerged as a much more prominent individual in the overall family operations," read one telex.

D'Elia was one of the few remaining members of the Bufalino hierarchy who wasn't dead or in prison. Hit-man Jack Parisi died in December 1982 of natural causes, as did capo Philip Medico, who passed in February 1983. Bufalino's closest friend, Casper "Cappy" Giumento, died of natural causes in March 1987. And Steven LaTorre, one of the original Men of Montedoro, passed away in July 1984. He was ninety-eight years old.

Along with Bufalino, among those imprisoned were James Osticco, who was sentenced to eight years for obstruction of justice for fixing the 1977 Louis DeNaples' trial. Osticco and Casper Guimento were also charged in July 1983 with supplying dynamite from Medico Industries to Frank Sheeran and hit man Charles Allen. In poor health, he was released in 1988 and died two years later. Frank Sheeran was sentenced to eighteen years in federal prison after he was charged in 1980 with mail fraud, labor racketeering and taking bribes. Consigliere Edward Sciandra was charged with failing to report income tax and sentenced to two consecutive eighteen-month terms. Capo Anthony Guarnieri, who with Billy D'Elia handled many of the important assignments, was sentenced to thirty years in prison in 1989 for a variety of offenses, including labor racketeering and conspiracy.

The RABFAM investigation was finally shut down in December 1983 but not before it documented the Bufalino family at the height of its power. D'Elia and Guarnieri, with Bufalino's blessing, expanded the family's stake in Nevada, taking control of the Edgewater Hotel and Casino in Laughlin, Nevada, following meetings with Tony Spilotro, the Chicago mobster whose violent life was portrayed by Joe Pesci in Martin Scorsese's 1995 film *Casino.*

D'Elia and Guarnieri also opened new channels with the Lucchese crime family in New York. The family was also doing business outside of its traditional territories in Baltimore and Miami.

When the FBI finally closed the RABFAM investigation, the agency credited the probe with "decimating" the Bufalino family, touting how "the most significant members of the Russell A. Bufalino LCN Family have been convicted or are in the early stages of judicial proceedings."

Truth be told, most of the successful prosecutions came outside of RABFAM's circle. Bufalino, for instance, was prosecuted by the U.S. attorney in New York. Nevertheless, RABFAM did provide the Justice Department with reams of intelligence on the Bufalino family, and as the family shrunk, so too did its national prestige.

But not until Russell Bufalino's long tenure as a mob boss officially ended, in 1989, after he suffered a stroke. Wheelchair bound, he was transferred to the federal medical facility at Springfield, Missouri. It was there that he was reunited with Frank Sheeran, who suffered from severe arthritis and had been sent to Springfield to finish out his sentence. Though confined to a wheelchair, Bufalino enjoyed playing bocce and eating ice cream. He also attended mass regularly, something he had done on and off most of his life.

Bufalino had always been known as the Quiet Don. He eschewed many of comforts enjoyed by his contemporaries, who opted for fine Italian silk suits, flashy cars and large, often ostentatious homes. Bufalino preferred to live in the shadows and behind the scenes. For him, living modestly, at least in public, was just good business, something he learned long ago from the first Sicilians to arrive in the United States.

Following his release from prison, in 1991, Bufalino was moved into a nursing home near Scranton, where he was treated royally. When visitors came by to pay their respects, they stopped at the front of his bed and kissed his feet.

Russell Bufalino died of natural causes on February 25, 1994.

# EPILOGUE

In the spring of 2010, I received an e-mail from a prominent figure in the Scranton–Wilkes-Barre area asking if I would be open to a meeting with an unidentified individual to discuss my work on Russell Bufalino. Few people knew I was working on a new book, much less one about the secretive Bufalino, but word apparently spread to certain corners. When I asked who I would be meeting with, I was told the individual's identity would be revealed at the time of the meeting.

Call me inquisitive or just stupid, but I agreed to the meeting, and in June 2010, I drove to an office midway between Scranton and Wilkes-Barre. There, the person who e-mailed me greeted me warmly and then led me to a back office. When the door opened, an older man emerged. He introduced himself, and I immediately recognized his last name.

Lunch had already been ordered, and we sat down to eat. After some small talk, the person who handled the introductions excused himself and closed the door, leaving me with the businessman.

The reason for the meeting, he said, was to get a feel for what I was working on and to see if he could help in any way. He explained that long ago he had some dealings with Russell Bufalino and that Bufalino remained a person of great interest to him. The individual also said he knew Louis DeNaples. I explained there wasn't much I was going to say on that topic. My interest, and apparently the businessman's, was Bufalino, and amid promises to introduce me to several old Bufalino cronies, the inevitable question emerged.

"Have you spoken to Billy D'Elia?"

D'Elia was imprisoned at the time at a federal facility near Los Angeles and wasn't due to be released until 2013. But he had been cooperating with the federal and state authorities and the businessman wanted to know if he, in fact, was cooperating with me.

"He's someone you should definitely talk to," he said.

The businessman looked at me closely.

"All I can tell you is that I'm open to interviewing anyone who knew Russell Bufalino," I said.

"So you've spoken to him?"

"I didn't say that. All I'm saying is I would be open to speaking to anyone who knew Russell Bufalino."

I did speak to a number of people familiar with the life of Russell Bufalino, and they were reliable sources for some of the information contained in the book, such as

Bufalino's relationship with Cuban dictator Fulgencio Batista and universal confirmation of Frank Sheeran's account of the murder of Jimmy Hoffa.

As we continued our discussion, the businessman said a book on Bufalino would make a few people nervous, people whom he described as "sleepers." They were men, around his age, he said, who had made their marks as legitimate, successful businessmen or professionals but who remained part of the old Bufalino family.

"These are people who under no circumstances want to be identified," he said.

We ended the meeting shaking hands and agreeing to talk again. The businessman was going to introduce me to several people who knew Bufalino, and I was going to send him a copy of my Sammy Davis Jr. book, *Deconstructing Sammy*. The businessman, it turned out, was a Sammy fan.

I've often thought about that early conversation.

Trying to tell the story of Russell Bufalino was a difficult task. There are but a handful of people still alive who can say they knew him, and because of his secretive nature, there wasn't much in the way of personal documentation. Old news clippings from the local papers reported on his arrests, but they had never taken a hard look at the man or his business dealings.

Aside from interviews, I relied on information culled from the thousands of pages of documents I obtained, including FBI reports, police records, U.S. government committee findings and a host of other print sources.

What's remarkable, aside from the fact that Bufalino

was by far one of the most important Mafiosi of his time, was that the corrupt legacy he left behind continues to play a real and important role in the lives of millions of people. The political and legal drama that played out in the casino licensing was just one prime example.

Like Bufalino before him, Louis DeNaples relied on the support of a bevy of friendly local, state and federal elected officials in his bid for a slots license. Time and time again, people outside Pennsylvania shook their heads in disbelief, each time questioning some new disturbing revelation asking how or why something like that could happen. How could the courts look the other way? Where is law enforcement?

It reminded many of the old-timers of the days when Russell Bufalino could call on any number of eager politicos or police to fix a ticket or quash an investigation. Or how politicians wouldn't miss Bufalino's annual banquets. DeNaples can be seen as a student of Bufalino and merely following a road map drawn by his old friend, a road well traveled that brought riches to a few but one that left an entire region in a virtual state of depression. Blue-collar enclaves in a rural corner of a blue-collar state that has its own set of morals and operates in a sort of vacuum ignorant to nor even caring of outside opinion. A perfect example is Thomas Marino, the former U.S. attorney in Scranton who provided a personal reference for Louis DeNaples' gaming application but was later forced to resign in 2007 in disgrace. Marino was rewarded by DeNaples with a high-paying job, then later resigned in 2010 to run for Congress. Few outside of Pennsylvania gave Marino, a Republican, much hope, given the bad publicity he received resulting from his resignation. It didn't matter. Marino won the election by a wide margin. And if anyone thought that was a fluke, Marino was re-elected in 2012.

Just before the election, in October 2012, Billy D'Elia was released from prison and sent to live in a halfway house. Now sixty-five years old, the last and closest link to Russell Bufalino spent Thanksgiving inside Bufalino's old house in Kingston. D'Elia's son, whom he named Russell, now lived in the small ranch-style home. It had been left to him by Bufalino's wife, Carrie, who died in 2006. The couple never had any children of their own, and the younger D'Elia was named a beneficiary.

Two weeks after Thanksgiving, D'Elia's former protégé, Frank Pavlico, was found dead inside his home from an apparent suicide. Police said he had hung himself. Pavlico had been in and out of trouble much of his adult life, engaging in one real-estate or investment scam after another. He escaped a lengthy prison sentence for money laundering in 2006 after agreeing to wear a wire and record D'Elia admitting to several offenses, including the planned murder of a drug dealer. Pavlico served less than a year. He and D'Elia were longtime associates and said to be very close, perhaps even cousins. With D'Elia's encouragement, Pavlico had also testified before the grand jury that investigated Louis DeNaples, offering information on business dealings between D'Elia and DeNaples.

I knew Frank Pavlico. We had many conversations while I was covering the DeNaples saga for the *Morning*

*Call.* He had reached out to me after reading a story I had written, and we met several times at out-of-the-way diners throughout the Wyoming Valley. I really didn't know what to make of him. He was a weightlifter who drove a Land Rover and told stories of growing up with "Uncle Louie" and "Uncle Billy" and how everyone owed their livelihoods to Russell Bufalino. When I asked about his own businesses, he'd talk about these "great investments" he had and try to talk me into plunking down money. The police didn't like him, convinced he was nothing more than a serial liar.

I'm sure that at the time of Pavlico's premature death, D'Elia and DeNaples liked him even less.

Still, I was surprised to hear about his demise, though I have to admit I was somewhat surprised that he actually took his own life. He had been in court the day before after a warrant was issued for his arrest for skipping out of a hearing in South Carolina relating to another investment scam he was running. It was just another arrest for a man who was familiar with the inside of a jail cell and didn't seem like something that would lead a man to kill himself. He was only forty-three years old.

Louis DeNaples remains one of the richest and most influential men in Pennsylvania. His continuing battle with federal regulators over ownership of the First National Community Bank after he was ordered to resign as chairman in April 2012 and divest his bank shares took a fortuitous turn when the U.S Court of Appeals for the District of Columbia vacated the ban in January 2013.

His children continue to control the Mount Airy Casino Resort, which is the lowest-revenue-producing casino in the state. Original plans to build a vast retail outlet never materialized, though construction on a new pool began in March 2013.

Governor Ed Rendell finally left office in 2010. Aware that he could have been an eventual target of the Dauphin County grand jury, Rendell had remained mostly silent during the casino controversy. He went back to his old Philadelphia law firm, Ballard Spahr, and appears on local television as a commentator on Philadelphia Eagles postgame programs.

The law enforcement officials who spent years investigating DeNaples, D'Elia, Sica and others had also moved on. Although district attorney Ed Marsico and his lieutenant Fran Chardo continue as prosecutors in Dauphin County, state police trooper Rich Weinstock requested a transfer to a barracks near Scranton, where he drives a police cruiser and hands out speeding tickets on I-81. Dave Swartz remains with the Organized Crime Task Force.

Former state police commissioner Jeffrey Miller is now a vice president in charge of security for the National Football League in New York, while Ralph Periandi, the former deputy commissioner who initiated the investigation in 2005, is the head of security for Reading Hospital. Despite his thirty-two-year career as a member of the Pennsylvania State Police, Periandi still finds it hard to comprehend the apparent breadth and depth of the gaming conspiracy, and the inability of prosecutors to send even one person to prison.

Federal authorities continue to tout their prosecution of Billy D'Elia as a watershed moment that finally put an end to the Bufalino crime family. They may be right. But if you take into account what the elderly businessman told me about the "sleepers"—Bufalino men who live as legitimate businessmen and community leaders—then the Bufalino family is far more alive and powerful than ever before, and the legacy of the Quiet Don continues to live on.

# SOURCES

This book is the result of six years of reporting that produced dozens of stories on actual events from personal coverage, first-person interviews with dozens of participants and a careful review of countless documents, including but not limited to FBI files, U.S. House Select Committee on Assassinations reports, Pennsylvania Crime Commission reports, and the original New York State Attorney General's special investigative 1958 report on Apalachin, New York.

Other source material included "The Men of Montedoro: Mafia in Northeastern Pennsylvania" (*Informer*, 2011); *I Heard You Paint Houses* (Steerforth, 2004); "The Garment Jungle" (*Reader's Digest*, 1957); "Meadow Soprano on Line 1!" (*Vanity Fair*, 2009); and "Pennsylvania Gaming-Panel Chief Faces New Flap" (*Philadelphia Daily News*, 2004).